MW01633086

It's Not Brain Surgery!

SIMPLE TIPS TO GETTING A GRIP ON A MORE SUCCESSFUL LIFE

Kimberly Alyn

ISBN 0-7414-3373-7

Published by:

INFINITY
PUBLISHING.COM

1094 New DeHaven Street, Suite 100
West Conshohocken, PA 19428-2713
Info@buybooksontheweb.com
www.buybooksontheweb.com
Toll-free (877) BUY BOOK
Local Phone (610) 941-9999
Fax (610) 941-9959

Printed in the United States of America

Printed on Recycled Paper

Published July 2006

Dedication

This book is dedicated to the inspiration of my life. I spent too many years of my life under my own leadership and direction, and it got me nowhere. It wasn't until I laid down my weapons, my pride, and my own agenda that I learned what it really meant to follow someone. This book is dedicated to my mentor, my role model, my leader. This book is dedicated to Jesus Christ, AKA, my JC! I've fallen on my face in life and you led me to renewal and restoration. You rebuilt me and put my feet on the right path. May I never waiver again from the amazing power of your leadership in my life!

About the Author

Kimberly Alyn is a sarcastic humorist, an author, and a professional keynote speaker. Her style is motivational, inspirational, and sarcastic. She provides self-improvement tips with laughter and sarcasm! Her hilarious stories and "tell it like it is" approach are over the top and people love it.

Kim tackles topics that every person and every business can relate to—the topics that everyone thinks about but few are brave enough to talk about. The universal principals of successful living are seen in a whole new light when Kim takes the stage! Her popular keynote address is taken from this very book.

Writing is one of Kim's passions. She is the author of ***How to Deal With Annoying People*** (with Bob Phillips, Ph.D.), ***101 Leadership Reminders, Public Speaking is Not for Wimps, My Favorite Sarcastic Sayings***, ***Annoying People and Why You're One of Them, Soar,*** and ***Pillars of Success*** (with former Secretary of State General Alexander Haig as one of the contributors).

In her spare time, Kim enjoys flying, motorcycle riding, drawing, reading, and writing. Kim also likes to spend time with family and friends engaging in outdoor activities. Kim believes in living life to the fullest as she strives to be a better person every day.

Contents

Introduction

I have never been one for long introductions in my books. When I pick up a book and have to thumb through pages and pages of an introduction, I can't help but think, "Geez! Does your train of thought have a caboose?!" I believe in getting to the point.

The principles of success are no secret. They have been around for thousands of years. We just need to be reminded of them, and sometimes a good kick in the butt is just what we need!

This book is NOT intended to make you feel better about yourself. It's intended to make you uncomfortable enough to do something about your life. Yes I'm sarcastic. Yes I'm blunt and to the point. If that offends you—quit being a baby and get over it! Lighten up and have some fun with it. You might just find some valuable things in here if you look closely....

Kimberly Alyn

By the Way

Just one small "by the way" before you get into the thick of the book... I will let you know where most of my "statistics" come from (unless I make them up—you may not know this, but 88% of all statistics are made up on the spot). However, I won't go to great lengths to provide insignificant details like the page number. We live in an Internet society, and you can go look it up yourself if you are so inclined. I have better things to do with my time. Besides, how many books have you read where you went and looked up a citation from the back of the book? My guess is NEVER! If you want to complain about it, please write your comments in the box below, rip out the page and mail it to me. Oh, and please write legibly.

Defining Success

Success is defined by so many people so very differently. Some people equate power to success. Some associate money with success. Others may look at someone who has stored up a wealth of material assets as successful.

The entire premise of this book is based on my own personal definition of success: ***"Using your God-given gifts and talents to fulfill your God-given purpose in life."*** The thirteen tips in this book all circle around that concept. If that is not a definition you can accept and build from, you may want to take this book back and get a refund before you spill something on it. If you haven't purchased it yet, you may want to put it down now and go find another book to thumb through as you finish your over-priced cup of cappuccino. Otherwise, we actually have somewhere to go together if we can at least start with a basic agreement on what constitutes success.

You see, if you can change your paradigm of what success really is, you'll discover that prosperity follows. Success is not about achieving all of your dreams.

Average people fulfill their dreams, but successful people fulfill their purpose. When your priority shifts from financial gain to fulfilling your purpose with passion, you can't help but be successful. When you follow the time-tested, proven principals of success, things tend to fall into place.

The principals of success have been around since the beginning of time. They are time-tested concepts that are not negotiable. Believe me, I have tried to negotiate them at different times in my life, and I have failed.

Many people have heard the story of David and Goliath. David was known as a brave young boy who took on the giant and conquered him! David went on to become an amazing soldier who commanded huge armies of men and he eventually became a king.

Average people fulfill their dreams; successful people fulfill their purpose.

After rising to what would seem like the peak of his success, David decided to negotiate the principals of success and do things his own way. He committed adultery and arranged a murder. This is what we refer to in the corporate world as the ultimate derailing! Consumed with self, numb to wisdom, and defiant of rules, David fell on his face. It wasn't until he realigned himself with his purpose and his maker that he was able to reestablish the success in his life.

Some of the most successful people in the world have also experienced some of the biggest failures. Even after devastating failure, you can still rise to success as long as you are willing to change your life and make different choices. The key is to learn from mistakes—you only totally fail when you learn nothing.

No one is immune to the rules of successful living. We have all made mistakes, and we have all fallen on our face (if you haven't, you will!). We can all identify with David as a result of our thoughts or deeds. I know I can, and without the realignment with my purpose and my maker, I would remain in failure. Many people do just that. They either remain chained to their past mistakes, or they live in toxic bitterness because of the mistakes of others. Life is very short and getting shorter by the second—don't waste it!

I am thankful God allows us the opportunity to put our failures and mistakes in the past and move forward. This is the starting point to living a successful life. If you're the kind of person who lives in the past, this book is not for you. If you're the kind of person who believes in clean slates and new starts, then my friend, it's time to begin!

1

We're Not Here to Suck Air—

Get Some Purpose!

I was at a social gathering once having a heated conversation with someone I would call "an angry white woman." She was pontificating about how messed up her life was, how terrible America was, and how pointless the world was. Maybe her fifth drink was talking, but it was obvious this woman had some anger issues.

So I listened for awhile and then I asked her a question: "So why are you here?"

"I love shrimp and pina coladas" she replied flatly.

"No, I mean, why are you here on this planet? What's your purpose? Where are you going in life? What's your vision?"

She made a constipated face at me and took one step back. She shook her head and laughed at me. "Are you serious? Who cares! My purpose is to be a slave for the company I work for. I'm on this planet to take up space. My vision is to get another drink—and where am I going? To the bathroom!" She walked away chuckling—she cracked herself up.

What a sad life! I have met plenty of people like this. These people have no idea what purpose they serve in life other than to suck air, work, and pay the bills. Some seem to make a career out of warming the cushions on a couch while living their lives through the television. They do nothing with their lives, put no effort into making it better, and yet are the first to complain about how messed up life is.

Come on people! Get some purpose! Most people spend more time planning their dinners than they do planning their lives. Having purpose gives life the meaning it needs. God created you with unique talents and skills, whether you use them or not. People who live their lives with purpose tend to make a difference in life. Sometimes it's small scale on a day-to-day basis, and sometimes it's large scale where a difference is made for generations to come.

> *"If you chase two rabbits, both will escape."*
> *—Unknown*

If you get in your car and start driving, you normally have somewhere you want to go. You have purpose. Your efforts behind the wheel of the car have meaning. You have a destination. Otherwise, you're just another aimless idiot taking up space on an already crowded freeway! Who needs that?

When you look at your life, you should have somewhere you want to go. You should have some purpose and direction. It's a crowded planet, and continuing to fill it with more aimless people isn't doing any of us any good. We have plenty of those already.

When I'm driving, sometimes I check out mentally and start thinking about things other than where I am going, and I realize I passed my turn or I'm now twenty miles past the LA airport when my flight leaves in forty minutes! That's life people. If you spend your time thinking about things other than where you need to be and how you need to get there, you may never arrive at your destination! Or you'll be extremely late getting there. I've seen too many people who never figured out how to be successful until they were well into their sixties. Well that's just crazy. There's no reason why you can't make it happen sooner than later, unless you're just mentally checking out and not paying attention!

> *"Purpose is what gives life a meaning."*
> *—Charles H. Perkhurst*

If I saw you at a social event and asked you why you're here, could you articulate an answer that doesn't involve a fancy little umbrella shading the pineapple slice on the side of your glass? Have you even thought about your purpose? What are your skills and talents? Have you even explored the different possibilities? Just so you know, having the ability to tie the stem of a maraschino cherry in your mouth does not count!

DRIFTING TO DISASTER

When I was thirteen years old, I lived with my biological father in a small town known as Port Orford, Oregon. When I wasn't in school for the summer, he made me get up at 3:00 am with him every day and go salmon trolling on his fishing boat. I thought it was dreadful. He made me drive the boat while he brought in the fish.

We were out on the ocean one morning at 4:00 a.m. when I should have been in bed (just like any other morning!). There was a small craft advisory that my father chose to ignore. A storm was coming in and the fog was getting thick. We were miles out when the wind kicked in and the swell came up. Even at thirteen, I had become very proficient at driving the boat. I knew to take the waves straight on and not sideways to avoid being capsized. However, I had never seen swells this large, and they were getting bigger by the second. As our boat topped one of the waves, we caught some air and slammed down on the other side. My father was neither a kind nor a patient man. "Bleep, bleep, bleep Kimberly! You're going to put a bleeping hole in the bottom of the bleeping boat!"

He then instructed me to turn the boat around and head in while he pulled in all of the gear. I couldn't see ten feet in front of me. My heart was racing and I was gripping the steering wheel like my life depended on it! When we topped the next wave, I fell backwards and the wheel came with me! I was sitting on my butt on the bottom of the boat with the steering wheel in my hand and my jaw dropped open. My father asked me "What the bleep happened?" I stated the obvious: the wheel had come off.

As he struggled to get it back on, we were rapidly approaching a shore of rocks. We had lost all control of the boat and any direction it might take. The boat was headed in a direction I did not want it to go, and there was nothing I could do to stop it. We were at the mercy of the wind and the waves, and on this particular day, neither was too merciful.

My father yelled at me to take off my shoes and get ready to jump overboard and try to swim. There were no life jackets on the boat and I knew I would be smashed against those rocks like a rag doll. I prayed as I frantically removed my shoes. "Oh God, I know my Dad's a jerk, but please don't let this boat crash. I'm not ready to die." I looked up and saw my father removing his shoes. As we both stood up to jump overboard, we heard a blaring horn. A much larger boat was on its way in and spotted us. They threw us a lifeline and we were towed safely to shore.

That was one of the most terrifying experiences of my life. It was hard enough for me steering that boat where I wanted it to go in those extreme conditions. But then losing the ability to steer the boat at all made me feel helpless and hopeless. I didn't have a choice in the matter, but that didn't bring me much consolation.

People often live their lives as if they don't have a choice in how it gets steered. They just sit helpless as their lives "happen to them" and they drift towards disaster. Without a steering wheel in your life, you'll end up drifting in directions you may not want to go. You may find yourself in places you never intended on being. You may find yourself feeling helpless and hopeless.

What steers your life is your purpose. You need to have direction and intention. Otherwise, you'll be tossed around by whatever waves you experience in life. You'll end up in some job you don't want. You'll live in a town you hate. You'll drive a car you despise. You'll wake up one day and wonder how your life got to the point that it's at. Maybe you're already there. It's never too late to put a steering wheel on your life. Depending on how far off course your life is, it may take you awhile to navigate to where you actually want to be. It doesn't matter how far down the wrong road you have traveled—it is never too late to turn around. Continuing to travel in the

> *"No individual has any right to come into the world and go out of it without leaving behind him distinct and legitimate reasons for having passed through it."*
> *—George Washington Carver*

wrong direction only gets you further away from where you want to be!

PEOPLE WITH PURPOSE

When I look at people who have happy and successful lives, I see purpose. When I see people with purpose, I see the success that follows. Look at Walt Disney. This is a man who had a clear vision of his purpose in life. As you will discover, I reference Disney a lot in this book because I believe he is a model of success in many ways, not just financially.

Disney has moral fiber, strong ethics, and perseverance to be envied! He knew at a very young age where his skills and talents were and he pursued those throughout his life. Disney experienced many failures and setbacks, but he never gave up on that purpose. He started with nothing and built an empire of success in every area of his life because he knew his purpose. Disney was once quoted as saying:

"The inclination of my life — the motto, you might call it — has been to do things which will give pleasure to people in new and amusing ways. By doing that I please and satisfy myself. It is my wish to delight all members of the family, young and old, parent and child, in the kind of entertainment my associates and I turn out of our Studio in Burbank, California."

How many people can articulate the "inclination" of their lives? When you get to the point where you can articulate your inclination in life, you'll open doors to a future that has purpose! When you have purpose, you can focus your time on being really, really good at what you do. When you learn to be really good at what

> *"What mankind wants is not talent; it is purpose."*
> *—E. Bulwer-Lytton*

you do, you can learn to be the best. Walt Disney learned how to be the best at movie animations and theme parks. No one did it better than Disney, and that's why he was so successful.

Mother Teresa knew her purpose and calling by the age of twelve! Her talents were compassion and helping the poor. She knew beyond a shadow of a doubt that this was her purpose in life. With no money or financial support, she stepped outside the comfort of her convent and opened an open-air school for the children in the slums of Calcutta. The volunteers and financial support followed. She started The Missionaries of Charity, which has now spread all over the world. Mother Teresa's level of success in fulfilling her God-given purpose far surpassed what she could have ever dreamed of. She knew her purpose and she pursued it with passion. Her success was not in the amount of money she made, but in fulfilling her God-given purpose with her God-given talents.

Not everyone has a lofty purpose like Mother Teresa. There are plenty of ordinary people living extraordinary lives. These people are experiencing great levels of success in their lives because they know their purpose and they are fulfilling that purpose. Hey I know some people who understand that their purpose in life is merely to serve as a warning to others. And they fulfill that purpose with a great deal of enthusiasm!

> *"Above all be of single aim; have a legitimate and useful purpose, and devote yourself unreservedly to it."*
> *—James Allen*

Look around you. It's pathetic. The majority of people don't live their lives like Walt Disney or Mother Teresa. They live as if they have no purpose in life. There is no inclination or motto to live by. Life is just a series of pointless events that lead us from the cradle to the grave. What a sad existence.

FINDING YOUR PURPOSE

So how do you discover what your purpose in life really is? You can start by doing some self-inventory. What are your talents and skills? You were given those for a reason. Where do your interests and desires lie? You were given those for a reason too. Those two areas often align and that makes the process of discovering your purpose pretty simple.

You may have many interests and you may have many talents. Sometimes it takes trying new things to discover where your true purpose and passion exist. If you are not really enjoying what you're doing in life right now, you've probably not discovered your purpose yet. I owned a financial planning firm for over ten years, and for most of that time, I enjoyed it. But it wasn't something I really looked forward to or loved. It was more of just a job for me. I sort of "fell" into it as a career and then built my education around it. I felt like I was helping people financially, but I didn't particularly have a great skill for math, and I definitely didn't have a great passion for financial planning. Deep down, I knew this wasn't my purpose.

> *"We are not put on earth for ourselves, but are placed here for each other. If you are there always for others, then in time of need, someone will be there for you." —Unknown*

During the time I owned my financial planning practice, I had started teaching some adult education financial classes at our local community college. After I conquered my extreme fear in the area of public speaking (to be elaborated on in another chapter), I realized that I loved teaching those classes. I didn't love it because I had a passion for the topic—I loved it because I had a passion for presenting.

One day a colleague asked me, "Kim if you could be doing anything you wanted to ten years from now, what would it be?" I didn't even hesitate in my answer. I said, "I would be public speaking full time." He smiled and asked, "Then why aren't you doing that now?" I couldn't come up with a good answer other than the standard excuses: I invested my education in financial planning, I have built a successful business, I have too much time and energy invested, it would be too hard to start over… bla, bla, bla!

I knew deep down I had desires and talents in other areas, but they were too "risky" to pursue. When I was only thirteen years old, I loved to write. I loved English, and I loved poetry. I never pursued that love and instead just let life "happen" to me. It wasn't until I fell on my face in life that I started to evaluate why I was here and what my purpose in life might be.

> *"To the person who does not know where he wants to go, there is no favorable wind." —Seneca*

I began to take inventory of my likes, dislikes, interests, talents, skills, and passion. I started writing like crazy. It was therapeutic for me and I looked forward to it. I felt like it came naturally for me and it was something I enjoyed. I knew I loved public speaking, but not about finances.

I took the life-changing leap and I sold my financial planning practice and decided to pursue my passion and God-given purpose in writing and public speaking. How do I know it's my purpose? I have a lot of peace about doing it. I love it. I have a passion for it. My skills and talents continue to grow in these areas, confirming that this is what I should be doing in life.

If you could do anything ten years from now, what would it be? Why aren't you doing that now? Stop making excuses why you can't do what you love. When you find your true purpose in life, things tend to fall into place. Your life begins to make sense. You begin to see the impact you can have on others. You begin to see the meaning of why you're here and why you were gifted with certain skills and talents.

Take some time out today to inventory your life. Be honest with yourself. Write down your talents and skills. Ask others what they think you're really good at. Ask yourself what drives you.

Look at the direction of your life. Have you just been dangerously drifting? Do you have a plan or a target for where you want your life to end up? Are you aiming at your target with your actions? I like to go out to the shooting range and practice my firing skills. If I am missing the target, it's not the fault of the target or the person standing next to me—I'm not aiming right! Don't blame life or others if you're not hitting your purpose in life—you need to aim a little better!

Life is too short to waste on a pointless series of events that move you from the cradle to the grave. You were created for so much more than that. Take inventory of your life, your gifts, your talents, and your passion. You will find a correlation between your gifts, talents and passion—that is usually where your purpose is found. So get busy today! Find your purpose and pursue it with passion!

2

Do You Actually Have a Pulse?

Get Some Passion!

It's not enough to know what your purpose in life is. You need to have some passion. When I look at any successful person, there is a healthy passion behind that success. Realistically, I think everyone has a passion for what they do. The reason I think this is because there are two definitions for passion:

1) A strong liking or desire for or devotion to some activity, object, or concept
2) Prolonged suffering

Most people identify passion with the first definition. However, I think many people live out their lives and have a passion for life and their work by the second definition: prolonged suffering!

Look around you at the people you know. Aren't most of them in a prolonged state of suffering in their jobs, their relationships, and their life in general? That's ***not*** the kind of passion I am suggesting when I say "Get some passion!" I'm talking about the desire, devotion, and the love for what you do in life. It's not hard to find people with the suffering type of passion—it's everywhere! Personally, I'm sick of seeing it every time I walk into a business. I'm sick of people who hate their jobs. I'm sick of whiners who complain about everything and have passion for nothing. I'm sick of people who put the absolute minimum into everything they do whether it be their job, their marriage, parenting, relationships, or just life—it's pathetic and it doesn't inspire anyone!

> *"You never achieve success unless you like what you are doing."*
> *—Dale Carnegie*

PEOPLE WITHOUT PASSION

I'll give you a perfect example of this. I fly commercially quite a bit, and it's very normal to get flight attendants who just want to put the bare minimum in, get the flight done, and go home. Boy, that sure makes my flight nice! I have encountered so many snotty flight attendants (both male and female), that I have been tempted on occasion to tie them to one of the seats, keep the seat in the most uncomfortable upright position, put a screaming kid next to them, force them to listen to a continual recording of their monotone safety briefing, and then charge them $5.00 for a puny sandwich on stale bread! But that's just me....

Life without passion breeds contempt. The next time you walk into a major retail business, take some time to observe the employees. Sometimes it's obvious that they loathe their jobs. I actually had an employee tell me once that she hated her job while she was taking my money for a purchase. I asked her why she continued to work there. She shrugged her shoulders and said, "It's a paycheck." How sad.

I tend to be blunt and brash at times... ok, ***most*** times! When I go into a business and it's painfully obvious that the person hates his job, I will say something. "If you don't like your job, you really should find something else to do. You're hurting the company, you're hurting the customers, and you're hurting yourself." It shocks people. I don't care. I'm sick of it.

I've had people tell me, "Kim, you don't understand. I have the worst boss ever. This company sucks. All of the employees are miserable." Then do something about it! Work somewhere else! Stop giving everyone else control of your life. It's crazy. We live in a free country with free commerce, and yet people still act like someone has a gun to their head forcing them to work in jobs they hate. Besides, we spend more time trying to fix everyone else when we should be focusing on ourselves. We spend more time identifying everyone else's faults when we should be examining our own. We need to get that big lumberyard out of our own eye before we offer to help someone get the small speck out of theirs.

> *"I can't imagine a person becoming a success who doesn't give this game of life everything he's got."*
> *—Walter Cronkite*

Maybe if we put a little more passion and effort into what we do in our jobs and relationships, they would get better. Maybe if we took the first step and stopped waiting for everyone and everything else to improve, life would get better.

People without passion are doomed to a miserable life of mediocrity. Maybe you're satisfied with that. I doubt it or you wouldn't have made it this far in the book. I know I don't want to live a life of mediocrity, and for me that meant a career change. It meant a life change. It meant a paradigm change. It meant a heart change. It meant a "Kim" change.

You need to pursue your passion, not your paycheck. People who sacrifice their passion in life for the steady paycheck are missing the boat. I believe you can have both. When you pursue your passion, the paycheck follows. Passion and success go hand-in-hand.

It's nearly impossible to separate success and passion. You'll never be fully successful at anything you're not passionate about. If you don't get up every day and look forward to what you do for a living, you really need to find something else to do. No one is a victim, trapped in a job, or stuck in a life they can't change. You have a passion for something, and you need to find it!

> *Pursue your passion, not your paycheck*

PEOPLE WITH PASSION

When you meet people with passion, it's easy to see where their success comes from. People with passion have a charisma about them that makes you want to be around them. Their passion makes you want to buy into their vision and get involved. I mentioned Walt Disney and Mother Teresa in the last chapter. Both of these individuals had a tremendous amount of passion.

Walt Disney was strongly devoted to his vision for animation and a theme park that would rock the world. It was widely predicted that his theme park would fail within the first year. When you have passion for what you're doing, you're not easily discouraged. You inspire people around you. You are driven to achieve results.

Mother Teresa had a deep passion for caring for the poor. She didn't care if she had the money or the means. She had faith the size of a mustard seed and with her faith and passion, the mountains were moved. When people have passion for what they do, it shows in their love for life, relationships, and their job.

As I told you earlier, it's easy to find flight attendants who lack passion for their job. I have had the rare opportunity of flying with a flight attendant who did in fact have some passion, and she loved her job! I was on a long flight one day when this flight attendant started her safety briefing that is normally so boring, I'll read the barf bag before I pay attention. Well on this flight, we had someone who loved her job. She began the safety briefing by saying, "Ladies and gentleman, welcome to flight 5540 with service to Los Angeles California. If you're on the wrong flight, too late, the doors are locked. We hope you enjoy lots of smog and plenty of traffic."

She had my attention! I got out a pen and starting jotting down some of her comments on my napkin. Throughout her briefing she would go outside the box and say some off the wall stuff just to make it more fun. She said things like, "To operate your seatbelt, insert the metal tab into the buckle and pull it tight. It works like every other seatbelt and if you don't know how to operate one, you shouldn't be allowed in public unsupervised."

By now, she had the attention of every passenger on the plane. I watched and listened intently to see what would happen next. She continued... "There may be fifty ways to leave your lover, but there are only four ways out of this plane: here, here, here, and here." Her arms flailed in animation as she pointed to each exit.

The laughter started getting louder. "In the unlikely event that the cabin should lose pressure, your oxygen mask will drop down in front of you. Please secure your mask first and then assist your child. If you have more than one child, just pick your favorite." The laughter now roared throughout the plane.

"When the plane lands, please stand up before your seat belt sign is turned off ***if,*** and only if, you wish to volunteer for cabin clean up. Also, please be sure to gather all of your personal belongings before leaving the plane as any items left behind will be distributed evenly between the flight attendants." She paused for a brief moment and appeared to be thinking deeply. Then a look of discovery came over her face and she added, "***Don't even think about leaving your children***. We ***will*** return those! Thank you."

By the time she got done with her spiel, the plane broke out in applause. What a welcomed change! Someone who has some passion for their job and loves what they do. As you can see, that was one flight that left a huge impression on me and I talk about it when I speak. When you make a great impression on customers, they will spread your praises like wildfire.

> *"One person with passion is better than forty people merely interested."*
> *—E. M. Forster*

People will settle for a mediocre product just to get great service. People will continue to go to restaurants where the food is marginal if the employees love their jobs and have some passion for it. On the other hand, people will stop using a fantastic product if the service sucks. Nobody wants to be around people who hate life. People love to be around people with passion.

PASSION FOR FISH

Maybe you've heard of Pike Place Fish Market. Maybe you haven't. Either way, I'm going to talk about this organization. It's a fish market in Seattle Washington. I don't know if you have ever worked around fish, but what a gross job! How could anyone have fun at that? How could anyone have passion for what they do when they have to work with smelly fish all day? Well Pike Place Fish Market is world famous. They are not world famous because they have the best fish (even though they are well-known for fresh, high quality seafood). They are world famous because their motto is "Dedication to having fun and creating excitement while we work."

This place is hopping! It's loud, it's fun, and it's full of activity. Employees are shouting out fish orders and tossing huge fish back and forth while customers watch. They involve customers in the fun. They walk around and educate customers on fish. If the employees don't love their jobs, they do a darn good job acting like they do!

If you go to the Pike Place web site, you'll discover their philosophy (www.PikePlaceFish.com):

> *A few years ago, we at Pike Place Fish Market committed ourselves to becoming "world famous." We've accomplished this not by spending any money on advertising (we've never spent a dime), but by being truly great with people. We interact with people with a strong desire to make a difference for them. We want to give each person the experience of having been served and appreciated, whether they buy fish or not. We love them.*
>
> *At World Famous Pike Place Fish Market, we stand for the possibility of World Peace and Prosperity for all people. We believe that it's possible for a person to impact the way other people experience life. Through our work, we can improve the quality of life for others. We are committed to this belief. It's what we do.*

We adhere to a particular set of E.C.Ps (Essential Creative Principles). These E.C.Ps have made our company culture a model for other organizations. Our vision is to see companies all over the world make it their business to improve the quality of life for people everywhere. Our commitment is to make our way of operating available to as many organizations as possible.

I think the whole world peace and prosperity thing is asking a bit much, but hey, it's better to shoot for the moon and hit an eagle than to shoot for an eagle and hit a rock! This is a company that has never spent a dime on advertising! Customers advertise for them because customers love being around them. Why? Because they love being around customers. They have passion for fish, they have passion for their jobs, and they have passion for having fun! If these guys can figure out how to have fun working around fish all day, then I think anyone can learn to have some passion for what they do!

WHY PEOPLE LACK PASSION

> *"Life is either a daring adventure, or nothing at all." —Helen Keller*

People lack passion because it's safe. You don't have to reach or stretch yourself to be mediocre or average about life. To have passion for anything, you have to embrace a higher level of feeling, emotion, and commitment. When you commit to something, there are expectations. You expect more from yourself and others expect more from you. Well it's just plain easier in life to set low expectations so we don't disappoint ourselves and others. Sad, but true.

People also lack passion because they have become cynical about life. Maybe they have been burned in a relationship and just don't want to risk getting burned again. If they have a low level of commitment and passion for the relationship, it won't hurt so much when it all falls apart again. People have been burned in jobs. They have put their hearts and souls into something just to be taken advantage of and thrown under the bus when cutbacks are needed. Why bother putting themselves out there again?

Helen Keller once said, "Life is either a daring adventure or nothing at all!" Either give it your all, or give it up. Don't work in a job you can't give 100% to. Don't give 50% in your relationships—give 100%!

Lastly, people lack passion because they are lazy! It's much easier to be blasé about everything than it is to commit to a high level of passion in life. People are lazy when it comes to their job performance, they are lazy when it comes to their health, they are lazy when it comes to their relationships, and they are lazy when it comes to improving their lives. Laziness and excuses flood our nation, which leads me to chapter three: "Get Off Your Butt." So don't be lazy... read on....

> *"When you set yourself on fire, people love to come and see you burn."*
> *— John Wesley*

3

Get Off Your Butt

And Take Some Immediate Action!

I am amazed at how lazy people can be! I talk to so many people who want to see results, but they don't want to take the actions necessary to see those results. People just keep making excuses for why they just "can't succeed". They don't have the right boss. They don't have the right employees. They don't live in the right neighborhood. They don't live in the right city… state… country… planet. Then pick a different planet—go to Uranus! Just quit complaining, get off your butt (speaking of Uranus), and take some immediate action!

I see people sitting around all day dreaming about the way things should be. They need to get off their butts and take some immediate action! Everyone has dreams, but what separates successful people from unsuccessful people isn't their dreams, it's their actions. Dreams without action are nothing more than hallucination!

TURNING DREAMS INTO ACTION

How many people have you met with great ideas and great dreams? Plenty, I'm sure. I know I have. But there are few who actually act on those dreams or ideas to become successful. The ones who do, and see it through, are the ones who got off their butts and took immediate action.

Jay Sorenson was struggling financially to support his family in Portland Oregon. One day he spilled a hot cup of coffee on his lap because the outside of the cup was too hot. He didn't sue anyone for millions (like the moron who sued McDonalds for spilling a hot cup of coffee… and won!). Instead, Jay starting thinking of ideas. He finally came up with the idea of a cardboard sleeve that would fit around the cup and protect your hands from the heat.

So Jay borrowed money from his parents to hire a patent attorney and then went $100,000 in debt to produce the coffee jackets. He hit the streets, soliciting cafes and coffee houses. He paid his dues. He invested, time, money, and energy to make it happen. He went to a coffee trade show where he got orders from cafes. His hard work and effort paid off—orders starting streaming in. The sleeves have an average cost of .04 cents each and Jay Sorenson's company, *Java Jackets*, now sells between 20-25 million jackets a month! You do the math. He and his wife also donate a large amount of money to charitable foundations.

Many people have ideas like Jay, but most of those people just dream about their ideas or talk about them. What made Jay successful was taking immediate action to turn his idea into a successful reality. Sometimes it's just *that* simple! But most people would rather just dream. If they actually took action and failed, their dreams would be shattered. If they don't bother to try, they can continue to just dream about it and talk about while "holding on to their dream" and living in La La Land (yep, that's a real place—people go there often and many people live there! It's crowded and over-populated now....)

PAY YOUR DUES

If you want to be successful, you have to earn it. You have to pay your dues! The only thing society owes you is... NOTHING! Society doesn't owe you a job, and it's not the government's responsibility to fix the mess you make of your life. If your life is messed up, fix it. If your job stinks, quit. Just stop expecting everyone else to make your life comfortable.

We all have to pay our dues in life. We have to pay our dues as a child to get more privileges. We have to pay our dues as teenagers to gain trust and independence. It's not owed to us. We have to earn it. We have to pay our dues as employees before we get promoted. When you begin to do more than what you get paid for, you'll eventually get paid for more than what you do.

If you want to adopt the philosophy of never doing more than what you get paid to do, you'll have plenty of support. Many people would agree with that concept. However, if you look at very successful people, they didn't embrace that attitude. Successful people always start out doing more than they get paid for and eventually they get paid for more than what they do (which ticks off the people who refuse to do anything more than what they get paid for). To be successful, you

> *"Success seems to be connected with action. Successful people keep moving. They make mistakes, but they don't quit."*

have to get off your butt and give more than is expected of you in every area of your life!

I don't care what people tell you, you are not entitled to a job. You have to earn it. And when you get a job, you are not entitled to a 401(k) plan, or dental insurance, or a parking space. You are only entitled to the agreed upon wage for the agreed upon work. If the wage isn't high enough to pay for your health insurance, then work somewhere where it is.

Employers started offering fringe "benefits" like health insurance and retirement plans to attract employees. After years and years of this, more and more employers started doing the same to compete in the labor market. In our society, after someone has received a "benefit" for too long, it becomes a "right" or an "entitlement." There is now contemplation about forcing employers to provide health insurance for employees. As a business owner, I'm sorry, but that is not my job! My job is to give you a paycheck for the work we agreed you would do. That's it. Anything else is just kindness on my behalf and should be appreciated on your behalf.

I provided one of my employees with a car. Now if enough employers did this, would it be okay for employees to band together and demand that all employers provide cars for their employees? Where does it end? What if employers starting demanding that employees not work the agreed upon hours, but that they also give the employer a foot rub every day? This country would be up in arms! How absurd! Yet expecting your employer to give you anything but a paycheck is just as absurd. If you have talent, skill, and passion for your job, employers will be falling all over

> *"Laziness travels so slowly that poverty soon overtakes him."*
> *—Benjamin Franklin*

you and giving you benefits to keep you. You don't have to demand those things when you're good enough. And you're only good enough when you get off your butt and pay your dues!

So what does it mean to pay your dues? It means you have to start at the bottom sometimes. You have to work your way to success. You can't take shortcuts. Sometimes it takes time and you need to invest that time. You can't make a baby in one month by getting nine women pregnant!

My first job was flipping burgers at McDonald's. Paying your dues means doing trivial jobs that you might think are below you until you can get to where you want to be. I've cleaned out toilets, taken out trash, made cold calls, and licked envelopes until I wanted to vomit. It means coming in early and getting more done than is expected of you. It means taking responsibility for your success and not expecting others to make it happen for you. It means sacrificing some of your TV time to improve yourself and add to your skills, talent, and knowledge. It means not wasting your time on stupid things that won't move you closer to your goals. It means taking action!

STOP WASTING TIME

According to the A.C. Neilson Co., the average person watches about four hours of television a day. That means if the average person started watching the average amount of TV at the age of five and lived to be age seventy, the average person would have spent over ten years of his/her life in front of a TV. That is just downright ridiculous. I won't even go into the negative influence that the crap on TV has on you—I'll just stick with the issue of the colossal waste of time that it represents. Ten years!

> *"If you don't make dust, you eat dust."*
> *—Jack A. MacAllister*

And people wonder why they can't get ahead and they can't get a break. Well get a clue! Step away from the television and you will add years of available time to your life to reach your goals. People often ask me how I get so much stuff done. I always give the same answer: "I don't watch TV."

It amazes me that people would rather sit around watching a reality show of someone else's real life than to live their own. What is wrong with you people?! Don't you have enough drama in your own life that you have to be looking for drama in everyone else's life? Geez! If you need some drama, come to one of my family gatherings… we'll treat you to some good 'ole down home drama like you've never seen!

I hear people complain all the time about not having the time to better themselves or make changes in their lives. Successful people and unsuccessful people have the exact same amount of time available to them. The difference is how that time is allocated or prioritized.

And you can't "make the time" for something either. If you had the ability to make time, you'd be one very rich and famous person with a lot of time on your hands! Don't say you don't have the time for something. Be honest and real. Say you don't want to make something a priority enough to fit in your schedule. We all have time for what is important to us. If it was important enough to you, I guarantee you would make time for it!

> *"If time be of all things the most precious, wasting time must be the greatest prodigality."*
> *—Benjamin Franklin*

Have you seen the amount of time people waste at work? They chit chat too much or sit on their computers playing games or reading blogs. If you don't know what a blog is, it's the new craze: web logs. People log their activities or thoughts or rantings and ravings. Some employees use blogs to bash the companies they work for. I didn't want to be left in the technological dust, so I decided to put a blog on my web site. My blog says "People who sit around all day reading or writing blogs need to get a life!" (www.KimberlyAlyn.com)

A 2006 United States study sponsored by Websense revealed some interesting statistics about people at work. It showed that employees spend nearly 25% of their time surfing websites that have nothing to do with their jobs. Over 16% of men and 8% of women admitted to viewing pornography sites while at work. The majority of them said they accessed those sites by accident... yeah, sure you did! Stop screwing around surfing the web and do your stinkin' job already!

Do you know what else is a colossal waste of time? Sitting around and talking trash about other people. It's called gossip. It sucks the life energy out of you and eats up valuable time. Maybe you've heard the saying "Small minds talk about people, average minds talk about events, and great minds talk about ideas." Well if everyone would spend less time at work and at home focusing on other people and instead focus on ideas for improving their own lives, what a better world this would be! The only reason we talk negatively about others is so we can feel better about ourselves. We put others down to elevate ourselves. We feel small and insignificant in life and we need to somehow find value in who we are. So instead of improving ourselves and finding our purpose, we try to find value by comparing ourselves to others and determining why we are better in certain areas. We need to get a life! We waste too much time on crap like this.

THE ASSASSINATION OF MOTIVATION

People tend to put things off until the last minute, especially unpleasant tasks. Procrastination leads to the assassination of motivation. I read an article in Psychology Today that said success is often sabotaged by procrastination. Gosh, I hope those psychologists didn't waste $100,000 on their education just to make that deduction. No duh!

When you are motivated to take action on something and you procrastinate taking that action, your level of motivation dwindles. The longer you put it off, the less likely it is you will ever get it done. Additionally, the less appealing the action is that you need to take, the more likely you will be to procrastinate. Mark Twain once said, "If you had to eat two frogs for breakfast every day, you wouldn't sit around all day lookin' at 'em, and you'd eat the biggest one first!"

There are certain things we know need to be done, but we just hate doing them. For me, that was always cold calling. So when I got to the office, I would sit down, roll my chair up to my desk, and eat that big frog! After awhile, I got used to it and it didn't taste so bad. I just knew I had to get it out of the way, or I might never get it done and I would starve to death. Procrastination will prevent you from becoming successful in every area of your life.

Procrastination keeps people in a constant state of disorganization, literally and mentally. If you're always feeling behind or rushed because you pushed the limits on some deadline, you'll never make time for reaching important goals. People who procrastinate allow their lives to be filled with distraction. Did you notice I said "allow"? You're not a victim of distractions. In fact, most of the time you create them yourself.

> *"Procrastination is the grave in which opportunity is buried."*
> *—Unknown*

An example would be spending time going through email instead of working on a more important project. Another example would be taking phone calls all day and not focusing on a goal that needs to be met. Another example would be allowing a coworker to engage you in a long and drawn out conversation about the politics in the office and how you're both getting the shaft by someone in upper management. I could make a list of distractions that would fill this book.

When I have goals and objectives that need to be met, I take control over possible distractions. If I have set a goal to write ten pages a day, I turn my phone off, close my email, lock myself in a room and focus. I can check my email later. I can return calls in the afternoon. If it's important enough for me to get it done, I will find a way. It's much easier for most people to make excuses and blame their lack of success on constant distractions in their lives. Yet the people who are reaching high levels of success aren't free of distractions, they just learn how to manage those distractions.

There are countless articles and information out there examining why people procrastinate. Who cares? Stop doing it. I don't care if it's because you have a hard time getting started or you're not a morning person or you don't know who to call for help. Just stop procrastinating and take some action! Get motivated and get moving.

I was browsing the web awhile back and I saw this banner ad that said, "Stop Procrastination Fast the Easy Way—Only $29.99! ORDER NOW!" How in the world do they ever get business? Their target market is people who procrastinate and they're asking them to act "now." A procrastinator will bookmark the web page, planning to come back to it later but never get around to it!

You don't need to pay someone to tell you how to quit procrastinating. You just need to get yourself motivated and take some action. Don't wait for someone else to motivate you. Motivation is internal, and you need to motivate yourself. Most people need a good kick in the butt more than they need a pat on the back.

Better for you to give yourself that kick than have someone else do it when your back is turned. Figure out what motivates you and get it done!

GETTING STARTED

All of the time we spend should move us towards our goals and objectives in life. If you have a goal to have a more interactive and close relationship with your kids, watching TV with them will not move you towards that goal. That would be a waste of time. However, if you went on a hike with them and talked about their struggles with peer pressure at school, that would be moving you towards your goal.

If you had a goal to get a better paying job within the next twelve months, standing in the coffee room bashing your boss won't move you towards that goal. However, if you spent just one hour after work every day doing things like looking for job opportunities online, updating your resume, calling associates, or improving your skill level, you would be moving yourself towards that goal.

> *"Procrastination is one of the most common and deadliest of diseases and its toll on success and happiness is heavy."*
> *—Wayne Dyer*

So take just one action every day that you know without a doubt will move you towards the realization of your dreams, goals, and God-given purpose. Just one action. If you're really on fire, go crazy—take two actions. Multitask. And men, just so you know, reading while going to the bathroom does not qualify as multitasking.

Start by making a list of the things you need to accomplish or get done to reach your goals. Make a long and detailed list of actions that need to be taken. When you get up tomorrow morning, take one of those actions. Just do *something* every single day that will move you towards your ultimate goals.

This is my life everyday. I have ultimate goals and objectives and then I have day-to-day goals and objectives that will move me towards my ultimate goals. Those day-to-day goals require constant action. I have a huge tablet on my desk full of lists of actions I need to take today, tomorrow, this week, this month, and this year. I look at it everyday (except Sunday—my goal for that day is to chill out and I don't need a list to remind me how).

If I want to get a book completed by a certain date, I sit down and figure out how many pages I have to write per day and then I take the necessary actions to make that happen. That might entail getting up earlier some days when my schedule is full. It might mean staying up later other days. It might require putting off some less important projects until I complete the goal. The important thing is that I take the daily actions necessary to reach the goal, which keeps me focused. It would be easy to make excuses why I couldn't get the pages done one day or why I was too exhausted to hit the keyboard the next, but all the excuses in the world won't move me towards the goals I need to reach.

How much time do you think Walt Disney spent wasting? This was a focused and determined man who took action every day to achieve success. He didn't make excuse and he didn't use the adversity in his life as an excuse to fail. Disney once said:

"A person should set his goals as early as he can and devote all his energy and talent to getting there. With enough effort, he may achieve it. Or he may find something that is even more rewarding. But in the end, no matter what the outcome, he will know he has been alive."

It's actually very easy to take the necessary actions in your life to become successful. Unfortunately, it's even easier not to take action. Most people choose the easiest thing to do, which is to do nothing. If you want to be successful, you need to get off your butt and take some immediate action. The average person makes excuses. The extraordinary person makes it happen!

4

Do the Right Thing

It Goes Against Society!

When we stop long enough to think about what the right thing really is, it's not brain surgery. I was making a pancake breakfast one morning for my nephews. Jonathan was twelve and Matthew was eleven. They started arguing over who was going to get the first pancake. Both of my nephews go to a Christian school, so I thought this would be a great learning opportunity for doing the right thing. I said, "Boys listen. If Jesus were here right now He would say, 'Let my brother have the first pancake—I can wait.'" There was silence as they thought about it for a second and then Jonathan, being the older of the two, took the initiative. He leaned over to his brother, put his arm around him and said, "Matthew, Auntie Kim is right, sooooooo... ***you*** be Jesus!"

Well that just sums up society. Oh we know what the right thing is and we expect ***other*** people to do it.

We expect others to be nicer and treat us kinder and drive their cars with some stinkin' courtesy as we're riding up their bumper flashing our lights and honking our horn because ***they're*** driving like a jerk. What's wrong with that picture?

We constantly hear about the importance of good customer service, and you bet, it's important! But what a joke it's become! If you want to be successful in business today, it's not all that difficult. The expectations of the American people for good service, high quality, and competent staffing are at an all time low. The bar is just not set all that high.

While high and lofty value statements proclaiming the near worship of the customer decorate the walls of most business, reality falls short. Forget about worshipping me, I'd be happy if you would just stop talking to your coworker about your wild weekend and take my money!

> *"He can't solve your problem—he's not a customer service representative."*
> *—A Staples Manager's reply to my question, "Why couldn't the cashier just refund my money? Why did he have to call for a manger?"*

How many times have you walked into a business, especially large chains, needing a problem solved and had the luxury of having a front line employee actually solve your problem? Not very often! They usually have to call for a manager, and even then you're lucky if the manager can take care of it.

It doesn't impress any of us to have employees have to call for a manger, and yet this is exactly what the majority of businesses out there are doing, and it's just ticking people off! It's not brain surgery—just do the right thing. Solve your customer's problems. Train and empower your employees to think and make decisions at the customer level. Deliver the service you say you're going to deliver. Treat customers the way the plaques on your walls say you will treat them. If the service of most major companies even came remotely close to what their TV commercials promised, I'd be amazed.

BAD NEWS TRAVELS FAST

Let me tell you the number one reason why you need to do the right thing in business. Because if you don't, word travels fast. Unhappy customers talk to their friends. They talk to their business associates. They talk to themselves. They write their stories in books.

I have been purchasing Dell Computers for over ten years. In my opinion, they have the best computer made for the price. Having said that, they have the worst service ever! If you watch their commercials, you would think you could call anytime, day or night, and actually have someone answer the phone within a reasonable amount of time and solve your problem. What a joke!

I am not exaggerating when I say every single time I have ever called Dell technical support, I have had to sit on the phone for at least thirty minutes, and that's just the hold time! That doesn't include the amount of time switching me from person to person while they try to solve my problem. Many times I get tired of waiting and I just hang up in frustration. On one occasion, I put my headset on and went to work in my office while I was on hold. I decided to see how long it would take to get any help. One hour and eleven minutes later someone answered. That's just insane! I have politely

> *"Customers don't expect you to be perfect. They do expect you to fix things when they go wrong."*
> *—Donald Porter*

brought it to their attention on many occasions, and the response is the same as it is with any business: "We are really overloaded right now with calls," or some other lame excuse of the week.

People don't care what your problem is. Fix it! Hire more people. All we want to hear is, "I am so sorry. That is completely unacceptable. As soon as I get off the phone I will make sure action is taken to solve this problem." Stop making excuses people and do the right thing! Don't call for a manager, and don't cut me off when I am telling you my frustration. Listen and take action. It's that simple.

THE KING OF THE RIGHT THING

Let me give you an example of the King of The Right Thing: Nordstrom: a high end retail clothing chain with 152 stores in 27 states. Nordstrom has a reputation for incredible service at the front line. Easy service, no managers necessary. The employees solve customer problems and they do it right. I have shopped at Nordstrom for years, and I have never had a problem with their customer service. But I wanted to find out how good their problem solving customer service skills actually were. So I went rummaging through my closet and found an old pair of shoes to return. I didn't actually buy these shoes at Nordstrom, but I was going to try and return them and see how they handled it.

So I drove to the nearest Nordstrom and I walked in with my old beat up dress shoes and an attitude. I headed straight for the youngest front line employee I could find in the women's shoe department. Her name was Josie Malet.

I said, "Josie, I bought these shoes two years ago, they have never been comfortable, I don't have the receipt, I live two hours away, and this is the first chance I have had to come into this store to return these shoes." At this point in this type of situation, every customer deserves to hear just two words: “You’re stupid!” Because we are! We’re stupid sometimes. But do you know what Josie Malet said? The two words every customer ***wants*** to hear: “No problem.” She said she would return the shoes and give me the sale price credit for any shoe in the store. Just so you know, I did the right thing—I didn’t actually return the shoes. I confessed that I was just testing their customer service. We both laughed about it and then she had me thrown out of the store. I’m kidding! She had a sense of humor.

Now ***that*** is customer service. Josie didn’t have to call for a manager. She just solved the problem and she did it quickly, professionally, and enthusiastically. I want to give a company like that my money. Heck I just walk in to a Nordstrom store now and say, “Here’s my money. Just take it. Whatever you want to give me for it is fine. I just love you guys!” In fact, I am considering renaming my first born after Nordstrom.

Do the right thing and loyal customers will follow. Do the right thing and a stronger public image will follow. Do the right thing and financial and relationship success will follow.

THE STORY OF MOST BUSINESSES

Sadly, most businesses are not like Nordstrom. The following story more accurately depicts how most businesses operate and treat their customers:

One day a man was walking across the street and was tragically hit by a bus and he died. His soul arrived up in heaven where he was met at the Pearly Gates by St. Peter himself.

"Welcome to Heaven," said St. Peter. "Before you get settled in, we need to make sure you are committed to us. Thus, we give you every chance to compare Heaven and Hell."

"No problem, I pick Heaven—just let me in." The guy had a pretty good idea of both already.

"Well, I'd like to," Peter said, "but I have higher orders. What we're going to do is let you have a day in Hell and a day in Heaven and then you can choose whichever one you want to spend an eternity."

"Actually, that's not necessary. I've made up my mind...I'd prefer to stay in Heaven."

"Sorry, but rules are rules...." And with that St. Peter put the guy in an elevator and it went straight down to Hell. The doors opened and the guy found himself stepping out onto the putting green of a beautiful golf course. In the distance was a country club and standing in front of him were all his old friends. They were all dressed in tuxedos, beautiful women on their arms, and they were all cheering for him. They ran up and slapped him on his back and they talked about old times. They played an excellent round of golf where he got a hole-in-one, and that night they went to the country club where he enjoyed an excellent steak and lobster dinner.

> *"I could ask someone here in the store to order that for you, but it probably won't get done."*
> *—A Home Depot Employee on the phone with my husband*

The Devil, who was actually a really nice guy, came over and offered him a Cuban cigar. Then he and all his pals loaded into a limo and went to the most amazing dance club he had ever been to. He was having such a good time that before he knew it, it was time to leave. Everybody shook his hand and waved goodbye as he got on the elevator. The elevator went up and opened back up at the Pearly Gates where St. Peter was waiting for him. "Now it's time to spend a day in heaven my friend."

He spent the next twenty four hours lounging around on clouds and playing the harp and singing. He had a great time. Before he knew it his time was up and St. Peter came to him. "So, you've spent a day in hell and you've spent a day in heaven. Now you must choose your eternity."

He paused for a second and then replied, "Well, I never thought I'd say this, I mean, Heaven has been really great and all, but I think I had a better time in Hell." So St. Peter escorted him to the elevator and again the guy went down back to Hell.

When the doors of the elevator opened he found himself standing in a desolate wasteland covered in garbage and filth. He saw his friends were dressed in rags and were picking up the garbage and putting it in sacks. There were flames and horrible gases pouring out of the ground.

The Devil came up to him and put his arm around him. "I don't understand," stammered the man, "Yesterday I was here and there was a golf course and a country club and we ate lobster and we danced and had a great time. Now there's just a wasteland of garbage and everyone looks miserable." The Devil looked at him and smiled. *"That's because yesterday you were a prospect but today... well today you're a client."*

That's how it is. If I want to get a live person at a company, I hit the button for ordering and sales. They think you're a prospect, so they won't leave you on hold. But if you hit the number for customer service as a current client, you could wait forever. It's gross. Businesses should not have a toll-free number for sales or new customers and then a toll number for technical support or customer service, yet many do. What does that say to your existing loyal customers? It tells them you are more interested in impressing people who don't know you yet. That's gross too.

DOING THE RIGHT THING

Do what you say you're going to do. Follow through on your commitments and don't promise what you can't deliver. Give people more than they expect and you will gain their respect.

Be on time. Don't make time commitments that you can't keep. When you're late, you basically tell everyone that your time is more important than theirs. If you are habitually late, set every clock you own ahead as far as you need to until you start showing up to places on time. And if you can't make it to something on time (or at all), have the courtesy to call and let people know.

See your customer on time. It makes me sick how doctors think they can stack patients up in the lobby and make them wait an hour before even bringing them into the first holding tank! The only reason they get away with it is because people put up with it. I personally don't. I walk out and find a different doctor who is willing to see me when my appointment time is scheduled. Yes, there are actually doctors out there who will do the right thing and not overbook all of their appointments. It's rare, but it exists.

> *"Although your customers won't love you if you give bad service, your competitors will."*
> *—Kate Zabriskie*

Don't ask people to do something you're not willing to do. When I owned a financial planning firm, I had a few doctors for clients. I asked them what they would do if they made an appointment to see me and then I made them wait an hour in my lobby. They all said, "I would leave. I don't have the time to wait that long, and besides, it's rude." No kidding! So stop doing it to everyone else!

The major electrical companies and cable companies are like this too. "We'll have someone there between 1:00 pm and 5:00 pm." My reply: "Ok, I'll try to have someone there between those times too. If someone is not there when your guy arrives, just have him wait." They love that answer!

Do more than just "your job." Do the right thing. If the bathroom in the place you work needs attention, clean it! If you see trash on the floor, pick it up. It's petty and pathetic to not do those things just because it's not in your job description or you think it's beneath you. When I go to the movies and I use the restroom, I will wipe down the counter. If I see a cup on the ground, I will pick it up. It hasn't killed me yet, and it won't kill you either!

Don't forward people all that email crap, especially when they never hear from you otherwise. It's rude and it takes up valuable time to either just trash it or take the time to actually read the impersonal, idiotic, forwarded email. If you want to encourage someone or make them feel good about themselves, don't kid yourself into thinking that you pressing the "forward" button on some angelic chain letter somehow equates to a gigantic effort on your part into the relationship. Instead, pick one person a week that you know and sit down and type out a real paragraph to them about why you're glad you know them, what you appreciate about them, and the well wishes you have for them. ***That*** would be the right thing!

> *"Hold yourself responsible for a higher standard than anybody else expects of you."*
> *—Henry Ward Beecher*

Have some manners. Thank people for their kindness. Ask nicely when you want something. If you bump into someone, apologize. If someone apologies, forgive them. If you're walking across the street and a car is waiting for you, speed up! Show respect to others and drive with courtesy. Stop riding up people's bumpers. And if you're driving in the passing lane and someone is behind you and no one is in the right lane, **move over!** It's called a passing lane for a reason! Have some manners.

Return phone calls promptly. If someone leaves you a message, call them back within twenty four hours. If you can't, have someone else call them and tell them why. If someone is waiting on you for information, get back to them quickly, even if you don't have the information yet. Getting back to them and telling them you are still working on it instills trust and confidence. Don't make people follow up with you.

If you're in sales, give people what they need, not what **you** want them to have. Don't try to sell people stuff they don't want or need. I walked into a large pet store chain once and I told the guy I was looking for a little Jack Russel dog. He didn't have any at the time, so he proceeded to try and sell me a cat. I said, "Can this cat catch a frisbee? I don't like cats, I don't want cats, don't try to sell me a cat." My husband pulled me to the side and said, "Kim, geez! What is your beef with cats?"

I said, "Four things to be exact! Number one, they shed their hair all over the house. Number two, they're right up in your face when you don't want them to be and then they ignore you when you want to pet them. Number three, they want to be pampered all the time and number four, they are the pickiest eaters on the face of the earth!" My husband just shook his head and rolled his eyes. He said, "Honey, you just described ***yourself***!" I wasn't swayed. I'll never buy a cat.

Just do the right thing. When I owned a financial planning business, I was "independent." That means I didn't work for any of the big brokerage houses. The reason I didn't was because those brokerage houses make a market in certain stocks and they have their registered representatives push that stock on the clients. It may not be what the client really needs, but it's what the rep really needs to sell. That's just wrong and it's not in the client's best interest. Do the right thing. Don't try and sell people things they don't want or need.

I am amazed at how many businesses are now offering classes or having their employees take classes on ethics. You shouldn't need a class on ethics to know what the right thing is. If you have to ask yourself if a decision you are making may seem unscrupulous, it probably is! The lines of ethical behavior are very clear, timeless, and non-negotiable. Nothing is ever worth crossing those lines. If you make unethical decisions just to be financially successful, how can that be worth it? What does it benefit a man to gain the whole world if he loses his soul? The important thing in life is not what you gain, but what you become. When you become a person of integrity, you will gain all the right things.

> *"Ethics and equity and the principles of justice do not change with the calendar."*
> *—D.H. Lawrence*

Don't do unto others as you would have them do unto you. Instead, do unto others as ***they*** would have you do unto them. It might not bother you when someone doesn't call you back for days. It might not bother you if someone smokes around you. It might not bother you if someone doesn't say please. Know and meet the needs of others before asking them to meet your needs.

I was reading a book one day and the author said to do whatever it is that brings you pleasure, and nothing that brings you pleasure should ever make you feel guilty (like having sex with whoever you want was his example). What a crock! Some sick people in the world get great pleasure out of killing other people. It brings me great pleasure to eat tons of junk food, sit around all day and do nothing, and gripe about all the people who get on my nerves. But that's not doing the right thing. Doing the right thing is eating healthy, being productive, and telling people to their face that they get on my nerves.

Doing the right thing often requires denying your pleasures for the greater good (often ***your*** greater good). I've been down the path of self-indulgence, and it only leads to destruction. If you don't want to learn from my stupid mistakes, then fine, go make a mess out of your life. But if you want to circumvent all that and live a more successful life, then do the right thing whether it brings you pleasure or not!

Doing the right thing is what I call "Up Time," and it's time for *this* country to experience a little Up Time. So America, listen up:

If you see injustice, **STAND UP**. If something needs to be said, **SPEAK UP**. If you make an appointment, **SHOW UP**. If someone needs some help, **STEP UP**. If you're blind to your faults, **WAKE UP**. If you make a mistake, **FESS UP**. If someone else is talking, **SHUT UP**. If you make a mess, **CLEAN IT UP**. If you drop trash, **PICK IT UP**. If bad things happen, **SUCK IT UP!**

Folks, if you don't agree with all of this, well then you're just **messed up!**

**check out Kim's Up Time T-Shirt at www.KimberlyAlyn.com*

5

So You Think Life Sucks?

Get Some Perspective!

I am always amazed at how bad some people think they have it. We have all had adversity in our lives—some more than others. We all have our stories—some worse than others. I think we all need to get some perspective. It could always be worse than it is. My childhood sucked. I won't bore you with the gory details. The point is I could have used my childhood as an excuse to fail throughout life. But I believe the words of Charles Swindoll: "Only 10% of life is what happens to you; 90% is how you choose to respond to it."

A wise poet once said, "Adversity has the effect of eliciting talents, which in prosperous circumstances would have lain dormant." Tom Ryan said, "Never daunted, I shall cope with adversity in my traditional manner... with sulking and nausea."

We all have a choice in how we approach the inevitable trials and tribulations that arise in our lives. We can master our adversity, or be mastered by it. We can allow adversity to bring out the best in us, or we can sulk in it. The choice is ours.

AN ICE CUBE, GRAPE, OR JOSHUA TREE

A young man named Joshua made his final commitment shortly after the September 11th attacks to become a United States Marine. He was one of thousands of Marines who made the choice to put on a uniform, stand tall and wave goodbye to his family, his friends, and his sweetheart as he committed to stand in the gap for freedom's sake.

Joshua knew all too well the potential adversity he could face. But he armored himself with his best weapon at his side. It's not a rifle; it's not a grenade; it's not even a tank. Joshua armored himself with the hope of the Joshua Tree.

We all choose how we will respond to adversity. We can either respond like an ice cube, a grape, or a Joshua Tree. When all three of these are faced with the same scorching desert heat of adversity, they all respond differently. The ice cube starts out solid and unrelenting, but after facing the heat of adversity, ends up weakened and melted. The grape starts out soft and tender, but under the heat of the desert ends up shriveled and unrecognizable. But the Joshua tree flourishes in the scorching desert heat and the hotter the sun, the more it thrives. In fact, without the heat of adversity, it would die.

> *"Prosperity discovers vice. Adversity discovers virtue."*
> *— Mark Twain*

The Joshua tree can only be found in the Mojave Desert. It's a strange coincidence that the Joshua Tree National Park is located in 29 Palms, home of the Marine Combat Center where the Joshua of this story completed his training. Joshua and the Joshua Tree symbolize the hope and resilience that every Marine has had to face as their boots land in the sands of Iraq. Those men understand the heat of adversity. They understand that they may not be able to control everything that happens to them, but they can certainly control how they choose to respond to it. They can allow the adversity to weaken them like the ice cube and melt away their hope and their strength. They can allow adversity to take their soft and tender side (often hidden under their macho fatigues!) and make it unrecognizable as they shrivel under adversity like the grape. Or they can choose to use the adversity to strengthen them and cause them to flourish like the Joshua Tree.

> *"If you can't stand the heat, get out of the kitchen!"*
> *—Harry Truman*

Well Joshua spent seven months in Iraq, and he came back a stronger man for it. He allowed the heat of adversity to strengthen him, not weaken him. I admire his strength and resilience, and as his mother, I couldn't be more proud than I am!

If you're reading this book and you live in America and you think life sucks, you may need some perspective. We live in a country of freedom and riches. We have unequaled opportunity for success in every area of our lives. That's why everyone wants to come here. You don't see people digging underground tunnels the size of Texas to get into Mexico (or any other country for that matter). People want to come here because it's the easiest place on earth to become successful.

But sadly, we are a spoiled, rotten society of whiners. We have no idea what real adversity is, and no perspective on what a rough life really is. We sue people for tossing a T-shirt out to us in the audience because it hit us in the eye, it burned a little, and we were humiliated in front of hundreds of people! Whaaaaaa! Life is so dang tough! Get some perspective people!

A MAN WITH PERSPECTIVE

Some time ago I attended a conference in Palm Springs, California. My husband and I were wandering around the conference grounds in the late afternoon trying to find a place to get some food—just a snack to hold us over until dinner. We found one restaurant open and made our way to the elevator leading to the top floor. My husband held the door as a man in a wheelchair rolled inside the elevator car. I normally experience that awkward silence in the elevator, never knowing quite what to say. My husband, on the other hand, talks to everyone. He talks to kids, adults, friends, strangers... himself! I watched as he struck up idle conversation with this very kind and friendly man.

> *"If you are pained by external things, it is not they that disturb you, but your own judgment of them. And it is in your power to wipe out that judgment now."*
> *—Marcus Aurelius*

I studied his wheelchair as he looked up, smiling and chatting with my husband. His face and hands were badly scarred by what appeared to be burns. His hands were missing most of his fingers, yet I watched him maneuver his wheelchair deftly.

The elevator doors opened and he wheeled out as my husband held the door. I smiled and walked behind him as my husband invited him to join us for a snack. He graciously agreed.

We sat at a table together and introduced ourselves. His name was W. Mitchell, but folks just called him Mitchell. He was on the agenda as our keynote speaker for the brunch on the last day of the conference. I had never heard his story and I had never heard him speak. I knew he didn't want to spoil it for us by spilling his life story there at the table, but I was squirming in my seat wanting to ask him what happened to him.

Instead, we talked about life and public speaking, and ideas for the future. This man was full of humor, life, and love. I wondered if he had been this way since childhood and didn't know any different. I wondered how he had learned to adapt to life so well. I was curious, nosey, and impatient—I couldn't believe I had to wait until the next day to find out!

Well it was worth the wait. I sat on the edge of my seat so I could catch every word. I waited anxiously to find out the story behind W. Mitchell. It was not a story I expected. He hadn't been in a wheelchair all of his life. He hadn't been burned all of his life. He had known and experienced a normal, healthy, and spirit-filled childhood and adolescence. He was twenty eight years old and lovin' life! He was taking flying lessons and had just learned to fly solo. He was on cloud nine coming back from the airport on his brand new motorcycle when his life changed forever. A laundry truck cut him off and he smashed into the side of the truck. He slid with the bike across the pavement as the gas tank erupted and doused him with gallons of gasoline. The gasoline ignited.

> *"That some good can be derived from every event is a better proposition than that everything happens for the best, which it assuredly does not."*
> *—James K. Feibleman*

Over 65% of his body was severely burned. The leather jacket he was wearing saved the large area it covered and the helmet saved his life. Most of his hands were lost and his entire face was drastically burned. After awakening from two weeks in a coma, surgeons went to work attempting to rebuild his face and body. After thirty two sessions of plastic surgery and months of rehabilitation, he was released back into the world. Through trying and difficult times, he adjusted and began to rebuild his life. He knew that "It's not what happens to you, it's what you do about it" (one of his quotes).

Mitchell became a part owner in a commercial building and invested in a new design for wood burning stoves. Both proved profitable and Mitchell became a multi-millionaire. Life was good again and he had overcome one of the worst adversities anyone could experience in a lifetime. And you would think one would be enough.

Mitchell had continued with his flying and was a licensed pilot. He took a flight one day with three other passengers. During takeoff, ice on the wings compromised the airflow over the wings and put the plane in a stall, sending it plummeting back to the ground. The three passengers walked away from the incident. Mitchell experienced a severe jarring in his back and couldn't get out of the plane. He would soon discover that he was paralyzed from the waist down and would never walk again.

> *"The best way out of a difficulty is through it."*
> *—Anonymous*

Life's not fair. How can one person endure so much? Wasn't the burn accident enough? Surely this man would break now, curse the world, and give up. But he didn't. Instead, he continued to live life to the fullest. He married his nurse, ran for mayor, and became a public speaker. He now shares his inspiring story with audiences worldwide. His story should inspire you to stop whining about your life, let adversity strengthen you, and get some dang perspective!

TOMMY AND THE JUDO MASTER

Many people wallow in their trials and adversities. Quite often, people use their shortcomings as an excuse to fail. I know plenty of people like this, and it's a shame. The people who learn to use their obstacles as a strengthening tool instead of a weakening one are usually the people who succeed. They are the ones who refuse to become victims.

> *"I know God will not give me anything I can't handle. I just wish that He didn't trust me so much."*

Tommy was ten years old when he decided to study judo. His parents reluctantly agreed to let him give it a try. Tommy had lost his left arm in a devastating car accident, and his parents didn't want him to become discouraged at not being able to master Judo without two working arms. The judo master didn't bat an eye at training Tommy. All he asked was that Tommy do exactly as he instructed and stay committed to the training. After three months of intense training the master had taught him only one move.

Tommy finally asked him why: "Sensei, shouldn't I be learning more moves?" The sensei just smiled and said, "This is the only move you know, but this is the only move you'll ever need to know." Tommy couldn't help thinking that maybe the sensei had been sniffing a little too much wasabi. But, he maintained confidence in his teacher, and kept training anyway.

Several months later, the sensei took Tommy to his first tournament. Surprising himself, Tommy easily won his first two matches. The third match proved to be a little more difficult, but he used his one move and won that match as well. Still amazed, he advanced to the finals.

This time, his opponent was bigger, stronger, and more experienced than Tommy. The opponent looked at Tommy and started to mock his missing arm. "Hey kid, aren't you missing something?"

Tommy stood up taller and responded, "Yeah, as a matter of fact, I am—a competent opponent!" His opponent popped a fuse and charged Tommy full force. Tommy used his one move, and won the tournament—he was the champion! The crowd went wild! Tommy raised his one arm as he danced around the room in victory. He was undefeated.

After the tournament, Tommy and the sensei reviewed every move in each and every match. Then Tommy mustered up the courage to ask what was really on his mind. "Sensei, how did I win that tournament with only one move?"

The sensei looked him square in the eye and said, "Tommy, you won the tournament for two reasons... First, you mastered one of the most difficult throws in all of judo. And second, the only known defense for that move is for your opponent to grab your left arm." Tommy's biggest weakness had become his biggest strength. He had mastered the adversity in his life to become a champion.

IF YOU WANT PERSPECTIVE, LEAVE AMERICA

When my son was in Iraq for seven months, he saw things the average American will never see in a lifetime. He saw families living together in one small shack with a cement or dirt floor. He saw homes blown up by insurgents while families walked the streets with their belongings, hoping they wouldn't get shot. He saw combat, death, and destitution.

My son gained perspective when he went to Iraq. He saw a different world with different priorities and different problems. He observed for himself what a rich and powerful nation we have become in America and sadly, how spoiled rotten we have become with so little perspective on life. We just don't know what it truly means to struggle for life, freedom, and opportunity.

We live in the richest nation in the world with the most opportunities available to us and yet we are the biggest whiners on the face of the earth! Instead of reaching out to help others, we extend our hands and ask someone to fill it with something. We have lost all perspective.

WHAT THE WORLD NEEDS NOW

Yeah, love is all good and everything, but we need some perspective too! Life is hard sometimes. Get over it! Life's not fair sometimes. Move on! We have become such a fattened society of people with an entitlement mentality that we really think life sucks when in fact, we just don't have a clue.

I was talking to a fourteen year old awhile back and he was complaining about his parents. "They make me clean up dog crap, I have to take out their trash, and I only get to play video games for two hours a day. It's bunk!" I really just wanted to put a diaper on him and shove a pacifier in his mouth! Are you kidding me kid? When I was your age, I lived on a remote piece of property with no friends around, no electricity, no running water, and no indoor plumbing. I had to clear brush everyday after school and water my dad's pot plants. If I looked at my dad funny he would whoop my butt!

> *"Parenting a teenager is a lot like trying to nail Jell-O to a tree!"*
> *—Unknown*

Look at the mentality of teenagers today. They have very little work ethic, little to no respect for authority, and a pissy attitude about life. Why do you think that is? Personally, I think it's because we have become wimps as parents and not enough people are taking the time and energy to discipline and train their children much less give them proper perspective on life. They have nothing to compare their lives to, so they think they have it rough. If you want to give them some perspective, take them on vacation to a third world country and let them see how other people really live. Let them live it for a week or two... or a month.

So many people think they have it so rough. Imagine your government arresting you, torturing you, and persecuting you for your religious beliefs. Imagine living in fear that you could be killed for believing in God... or believing in a different God than the government tells you to. It's hard to imagine such a thing, but it goes on everyday in China and other countries that do not allow religious freedom or many other freedoms we enjoy. We just don't have perspective here in America. We are so fortunate, and we have lost sight of that.

> *"The difficulties of life are intended to make us better, not bitter."*
> *—Unknown*

We all need to learn to appreciate what we have. Instead of looking at how bad things can be, how about appreciating what you have. Be thankful that you have a job instead of dwelling on all the things wrong with it. Look at every area of your life this way. Whatever is going wrong in your life, something has to be going right. Focus on that!

It seems as though we all go about our lives trying to dodge adversity and the growth that comes from it. If you ever get the chance watch a butterfly try to work its way out of a cocoon. There is a very small opening that the butterfly must struggle and push its way through. If you snipped the opening to try and help the butterfly, it would emerge easily. There would be no struggle and there would be no adversity. Seems like the easy and smart thing to do, doesn't it? Well it's not. If you gave the butterfly the easy way out, it would spend the rest of its life walking around the earth with a swollen body and shriveled wings. It would never be able to fly.

God designed it so that the tiny opening and the struggle required to get through that opening would push the fluid from the butterfly's body into the wings and give it the strength it needed to fly. Without that struggle, the butterfly remains crippled for life.

We have become a crippled society of people with no perspective. We let people take the easy way out. We try to spare them from hard work, struggle, and adversity. As a result, we have too many people standing around with their hand out expecting everyone to solve all of their problems. They don't think they should have to struggle. The hard work and struggles that life offers give us the ability to truly fly. We need to stop clipping the cocoon for people and let them push their own way through the adversities in life so they can become what they were created to be. And as Forrest Gump would say, "That's all I have to say about that."

6

Get a Grip on Your Finances!

Be a Good Steward

I owned a financial planning firm for over ten years. In that time, I worked with a wide variety of people, helping them to plan for their future. I showed people how to invest their money wisely, get out of debt, save for retirement, and not depend on others for their financial stability.

I was amazed at how poorly some people managed their finances. I worked with surgeons, lawyers, and airline pilots who all made over $250,000 a year. Some of these people had nothing to show for it—nothing! One doctor was making $280,000 a year (in 1995) and had a $2 million dollar house, a beautiful pool, an expensive Porsche, a $50,000 boat, and a $400,000 airplane. His kids went to a private school, had the nicest clothes, newest cell phones, and their own laptop computers. This doctor had no money in savings, no retirement account, no disability insurance plan, and $20,000 in credit card debt. He was pushing 50 years old and wanted me to tell him how to retire by 60. Unbelievable.

Then I had a client who had made a modest income most of his life. He didn't live high on the hog, but he didn't struggle financially either. He simply learned to live within his means. Additionally, he learned to put away 10% of his income into long term investments starting at a very young age. He came to me for investment advice. He was only 43 years old and already had over $490,000 in a retirement account (in 1993).

WHY AMERICANS DON'T SAVE

It's not how much money you make—it's what you do with the money you make. We live in the wealthiest nation in the world with the highest incomes and the most opportunities available to us for financial success. Yet in spite of this, we save less than any nation in the world. The savings rates of Americans has declined steadily over the past thirty years and continues to decline.

> *"The ability to save a portion of your income is a good index of character."*
> *—Unknown*

The Organization for Economic Cooperation and Development shows the US savings rate in the mid seventies at nearly 10%. Today, that rate is down to 1%. What's next? A negative number I suppose, which wouldn't surprise me based on the spending habits and credit card debt of most Americans. Again, we are just becoming a lazy and apathetic society of people who will not plan for the future and then we expect the government to take care of us.

When you put America up to other countries in regards to household savings rates, we are an embarrassment! India is at 24% China is at 22%, Thailand is at 19%, Germany is at 11% Korea is at 10%, Japan is at 8% the UK is at 6% and the US is at 1%! That's pathetic! What the heck is wrong with us?

Well some would say "We just don't make enough money here! We are living paycheck to paycheck as it is... how can we save?" Well the average annual income in India is the equivalent to $500 a year in the U.S. with the highest income around $3,500 a year.

In the US, the average annual income is about $32,000. The poverty level for an individual in the U.S. is about $9,500 a year. That means the poorest people in the United States make more than the richest people in India and yet the people in India still save 24 times more than we do on average! Why is that?

It's because people in other countries understand true poverty and the necessity to save what you can when you can. They also understand that when money is tight, you have to forego some items that are not true necessities. Americans think cell phones are necessities even when they can't afford one! They think televisions, stereo systems, high speed access, and cable TV service are all necessities, when in fact they are all luxuries.

The reason we can't save is because Americans feel the need to dive into credit card debt every Christmas just to be sure their kids have the latest gadgets and technology, because heaven forbid another kid has it and the fragile self esteem of our child may be harmed for life!

> *"The only reason a great many American families don't own an elephant is that they have never been offered an elephant for a dollar down and easy weekly payments."*
> *—Mad Magazine*

Americans can be struggling to pay the bills, but then go out and spend hundreds of dollars a month on unhealthy fast food.

I have talked to people who complain about living paycheck to paycheck, scrimping by, and not having enough money. They are in debt and getting further behind every day. But some of those same people will allow every child in the family to have a cell phone. They will spend $400 a month on cigarettes. They will spend $150 a month on 300 TV channels and then spend most of their time watching two of them. We have become a spoiled society of people who do not know how to differentiate between necessity and luxury.

Americans need to stop spending money on things they can't afford. If you can't afford to pay cash for something, then you can't afford it. I had a client who was deep into credit card debt and still buying expensive name brand clothes for her toddler! Like that kid knows the difference anyway. When I suggested she change her spending habits, she was indignant. She was not going to have her child live as she had—embarrassed of the thrift shop clothes she had to wear. I couldn't help but wonder how embarrassed she was going to be a few years down the road when she had to file for bankruptcy.

> *"In the old days a man who saved money was a miser; nowadays he's a wonder."*
> *—Unknown*

GOOD STEWARDSHIP

Now don't get me wrong here. I see nothing wrong with having luxury or non-necessity items if, ***and only if***, you can afford them. If you have cable television and no savings or retirement plan then I think your priorities are screwed up! I don't care how much money you make—if you have nothing to show for it, then you're not being a good steward of your finances. And if you're not a good steward in the small things, you won't be a good steward in the big things. People constantly say how easy it would be if they just won the lottery or made more money. Sorry, but if you can't live within your means at a small level, you won't do it at a large level. People get raises all the time and they simply adjust their standard of living up to the new level.

People whine and complain that others who are already financially successful just get more money while the people who need it more have less. Well there's a Bible story that explains this phenomenon. The story depicts a man going on a journey. He entrusts his property to three servants. The story tells us that he gave to each one an amount that was reflective of their abilities. To one he gave a small sum. To the second he gave a medium sized sum and to the third a larger sum.

When the property owner returned from his trip, he called up his servants to give account of what they had done with the money. The servant with the large sum had put it to work and doubled his money. The servant with the medium sized sum did the same and doubled that money as well. But the servant that had the smallest sum did nothing. He buried the money and returned it as it was to the property owner.

> *"Do not accustom yourself to consider debt only as an inconvenience; you will find it a calamity."*
> *— Samuel Johnson*

So what happened? The property owner called him an idiot (basically) and took the money from him and gave it to the one with the largest sum. The moral of the story: do well in financial stewardship and you will be entrusted with more. If you suck at financial stewardship, even what you have will be taken from you and given to someone who doesn't suck at it. That's just a basic financial concept. If you don't like it, stop sucking at it and you'll find yourself with more.

WHAT FINANCIAL RESPONSIBILITY LOOKS LIKE

Again, it's not that we don't make enough money, it's that we don't manage what we make very well and we don't take responsibility for our finances and our future.

Let me show you what would happen if we became a responsible society of people who became good stewards and planned for the future. Let's see what happens when you start putting away 10% of your income starting at the age of eighteen. Let's say you took that money and invested it in stable, long-term investments averaging an 8% rate of return per year (long-term investments in the stock market have done well over that for the past 50 years!).

So let's say throughout your life, you changed jobs, got raises, and your income steadily went up. Let's just say your income looked like this:

from age 18—20:	$15,000
from age 21—25:	$25,000
from age 26—30:	$35,000
from age 31—40:	$50,000
from age 41—50:	$60,000
from age 51—60:	$65,000

If you took 10% of your income starting at age 18 and put it away earning an average of 8% a year, by age 60 you would have **$1,018,174!** You can tweak these numbers for different levels of income—it doesn't matter. If you learn to live within your means and keep your lifestyle down with your income and save 10% in long-term investments, you will be able to retire without help (if you start young enough). You will have learned to keep your standard of living where it needs to be.

Instead, most people just spend through life trying to keep up with their friends. They have no savings, no retirement, no nothing. They just expect everyone else to make up for their lack of planning through government programs. We need to take responsibility for our own lives, our own finances, and our own future.

I did not come from a family of wealthy people. I grew up very poor. I grew up surrounded by people who were on welfare and couldn't put milk on the table, but could afford $200 a month in cigarettes or alcohol. I was a single mom at one point in my life with two young kids, no child support, no alimony, and no government assistance. I didn't have a television, a stereo system, or nice clothes. I didn't have credit card debt either. I invested in my education and I invested in my business. I didn't waste money on things that I couldn't afford.

ABOUT DEBT

- The average American has over $8,000 in credit card debt
- The average credit card interest rate: 18.9%
- An $8,000 debt, at a rate of 18% interest, will take over 25 years to pay off and cost more than $24,000
- Over 50% of credit card holders only pay the minimum payment on their cards
- The average American household is solicited seven times per year by credit card companies
- Nearly 78% of U.S. households are deemed worthy by the lending industry (but over 90% of American family disposable income is now spent on paying off debt!)
- Over 1 million credit card holders declare bankruptcy each year

We have a very serious debt problem in America. Again, it's not because we don't make enough money, but because we don't know how to manage our expenses. You can go online and check all of my numbers if you like. They are scary, but true.

I think if you are in credit card debt you're not managing your money properly. People make excuses about flat tires, broken down appliances, and emergencies. Well if you had been saving 10% of your income all along, you would have a way to pay for those things. Instead, you end up putting them on a credit card and paying 18%-22% interest! You can either save the 10% voluntarily, or have it forced on you when an emergency or unforeseen expense arises.

> *"My problem lies in reconciling my gross habits with my net income."*
> *—Errol Flynn*

I agree with the concept that you should not be in debt. However, I personally don't think this applies to "investment debt." When you buy a house and have a mortgage, you are investing your money. That asset will appreciate in value over the long term, and you will get your money back plus growth.

When you buy a flat screen television with surround sound and put it on a credit card, you have an asset that will depreciate the minute you buy it. If you can't afford to pay cash for it, you can't afford it.

I know people who dump all of their money and then some into building a business. I have done this myself and consider it an investment as well. However, if you have a history of running up debt on stupid ideas, you might want to get a real job. Additionally, if dumping everything you have into a business venture doesn't pan out, you could be facing bankruptcy.

I will never support the idea of filing for bankruptcy expect in rare circumstances (a psychotic ex-spouse charged thousands of dollars in debt under your name and the financial responsibility does not belong to you, or you didn't cause it). I believe if you caused the debt, you are responsible to pay it off. I have seen people file for bankruptcy to stop the interest charges or get creditors off their backs, but they continued to pay off the debt until nothing more was owed. If you owe it, you have a moral obligation to pay it. In 1833 Abraham Lincoln dumped all of his money in a grocery business that failed. He declared bankruptcy, yet paid off the money he borrowed to start his business. If you owe it, you should pay it.

SOME IDEAS TO BECOMING A GOOD STEWARD

1. Give away 10% of all you make. This Biblical concept not only helps others, it helps you. It keeps you from becoming greedy and obsessed with money. It teaches you to be more generous. People often say they would be generous if they had more money. If you can't be generous in the small things, you won't be generous in the big things. When you give generously, you'll find it comes back to you ten-fold.

2. Save or invest 10% of your income. People can learn to live within their incomes. If you get a 10% pay cut, you have to eventually adjust your standard of living or you get yourself into so much debt you will eventually end up bankrupt. If you force yourself to take 10% of your income and put it aside, you will learn to adjust to not having that money.

It amazes me when people tell me that cannot afford to do this. When I was a financial planner, I heard people complain about this all the time. But once I examined their finances, we revealed that they were spending over 10% of their income on things they absolutely did not need. Expecting a company or the government to fund your retirement is careless, irresponsible, and stupid. You're not being a good steward of your finances if you're not saving 10%.

3. Diversify your money. Putting your money in a savings account earning 1% (if you're lucky) is just not wise. There are lots of options out there you can start with for very little money up front. Mutual funds are a great way to diversify your money.

4. Stay out of credit card debt. If you can't afford to pay cash for it, you can't afford it. Credit cards should be used for convenience only and should be paid off at the end of every month. If you can't do that, cut them up!

5. Prioritize your expenses and make a budget. If you haven't learned how to live within your means, make a budget and stick with it. Once you've put aside savings and taken care of the major goals and expenses, then you can have fun with what's left over.

6. Educate yourself more on this issue. Read books about money management. Take seminars. Don't be afraid to employ an expert to help you. There are lots of great financial planners out there to assist you in this area (sorry, I'm not available anymore).

> *"I have discovered the philosopher's stone, that turns everything into gold: it is, 'Pay as you go.'"*
> *— John Randolph*

7. Teach your kids this stuff! Teach your kids to be generous and responsible. Teach them to put aside 10% for savings at a very young age and it will become a habit they will carry with them for life.

Managing your money is paramount to successful living. It doesn't matter if you have much or you have little. If you can't manage it, you will eventually have nothing. So get a grip on your finances and be a good steward!

7

Look in the Mirror

Stop Looking for People to Blame or Sue and Take Ownership!

People who are not making it in life always have a reason or excuse why they are not succeeding. There's always someone else to blame. Many people find it too hard to just take a good, long look in the mirror and say, "Maybe ***I'm*** the problem."

If you are someone who is legitimately being discriminated against because you're a woman, a minority, a Jew, a Christian, or a Martian, then you have a reason to complain or even sue. However, I have seen far too many cases where this is simply used as a lame excuse why some people didn't get the promotion or the job, or why they got fired.

If you are not meeting the standards of performance, don't sue for discrimination. Admit you suck at it and do something about it! Improve yourself and your ability to do the job. Evaluate whether you are even cut out for what you are doing.

I was talking to a woman who was 4' 11" tall and weighed 102 pounds. She wanted to sue a fire department for discriminating against her because she did not pass probation. She said they just didn't want her to be a firefighter because she was a woman. In reality, she couldn't carry a man out of a two-story burning building and down a ladder to safety. She couldn't throw the ladder. She couldn't perform the minimum standards that were necessary to be a firefighter.

So I say "quit crying about it and find something else to do!" I would say the same thing to a 4' 11" man who weighed 102 pounds and couldn't perform these duties. By allowing someone to come under the minimum standards just because they are a woman or a minority just puts them at risk and the public at risk. People need to be honest with themselves and just admit that they may not be cut out for a certain job whether it's physical limitations, mental, or social. It's okay to face the fact that you suck at it and just move on.

> *"The man who complains about the way the ball bounces is likely to be the one who dropped it."*
> *—Lou Holtz*

I tried out for the girls' basketball team when I was in high school. I didn't make it. I was tall enough, but my coordination stunk! I was able to be honest enough with myself to admit that. I didn't try to sue the school for whatever lame excuse I could come up with as to why they were discriminating against me. I suppose I could have made a case for "out-of-state" discrimination. After all, the high school was in Oregon and I came from California, and no one welcomed Californians in that town! I could have hired some fancy shmancy lawyer who may have taken the case for free just to get the publicity. I could have made a royal stink about it and blamed everyone but my own lack of ability. But I didn't. I knew I stunk and I could admit it. I just walked away and tried something else.

MAYBE YOU'RE THE PROBLEM!

We have become a society of people who expect everyone to hand us everything like we're owed something. Well I say get off your butt and take responsibility for your own life. If you are consistently getting fired from jobs, it's probably not the boss—it's probably YOU. Do something about it. If your boyfriends or girlfriends keep dumping you, it's probably not them, it's probably YOU. Get off your butt and fix it! If customers are consistently complaining about you, it's probably not them, it's probably YOU. If you can't get along with anyone at work or at home, it's probably not them, it's probably YOU! Make choices to make changes.

People find it much easier to look at others for why they fail than to look at themselves. One of the best places you can be in life is to wake up, look at yourself and say, "My life is a mess and it's because of the bad choices I have made. I think I'll take responsibility and fix it." That's a good place to be and a very foreign place for most people.

PERSONAL RESPONSIBILITY BECOMING EXTINCT

It's getting easier and easier for people to shirk their own personal responsibility. Two young girls who were grossly overweight tried to sue McDonalds for making them fat. I've got news for you ladies, it's called *junk food* for a reason! Where is the personal responsibility? Should alcoholics sue alcohol manufacturers for making the substance? I'm sure that's coming... someone sued a bar for letting them drink too much. Someone sued a casino for letting them gamble too much. It's insane and it needs to stop! You would not believe the crazy lawsuits that are being filed by people who just don't want to take personal responsibility for their choices, their actions, or their lives. Let me share a few of those with you.

Doctors tell everyone who need to hear it: eat less, stop smoking, exercise more, lose some weight. Well that's exactly what doctors told a woman from Pennsylvania. She probably doesn't want her name mentioned, so I'll just use her initials. Kathleen McCormick. Kathleen was obese, smoked cigarettes, had high blood pressure, high cholesterol, and a family history of coronary artery disease. Yet she did not listen to her *many* doctors when they advised her to change her lifestyle.

> *"Ninety-nine percent of all failures come from people who have a habit of making excuses."*
> *— G. Washington Carver*

So Kathleen had a heart attack. And she survived it. Then she filed a multi-million dollar lawsuit naming several doctors claiming that no one did enough to convince her to improve her health. Kathleen, the problem is probably not the doctors, it's probably ***YOU!*** It's not brain surgery lady—take some responsibility for your life!

A California man tried to sue the Las Vegas Hilton and Mandalay Bay Hotel and Casino, claiming the casinos were negligent in allowing him to gamble away more than $1 million while he was intoxicated. Had he ***WON*** $1 million, do you think he would have given it back because he was drunk? I'm willing to bet $1 million that he wouldn't!

A woman who was a passenger in a car that got into an accident wasn't wearing her seatbelt. She was slightly injured in the accident but neither vehicle had insurance for her to go after. So instead of taking responsibility, she found the deep pockets of Mazda Motors and sued them. She demanded in excess of $150,000 from the automaker, claiming it "failed to provide instructions regarding the safe and proper use of a seatbelt." Someone who is too stupid to use a seatbelt should not be allowed to operate heavy machinery like a CAR! I wonder how long she peed on her toilet lid before someone told her to put it up!

A man was hit by lightning in the parking lot of an amusement park in Ohio. Most would consider this an "act of God," or "an act of nature." Not this guy's lawyer! "That would be a lot of people's knee-jerk reaction in these types of situations," his lawyer stated. The lawyer has filed suit against the amusement park asking unspecified damages, arguing the park should have "warned" people not to be outside during a thunderstorm. And should the park also warn people not to run with scissors? Give me a break!

Derrick Thomas was an NFL linebacker for the Kansas City Chiefs. On January 23, 2000, Thomas was severely injured in a vehicle accident. Thomas lost control of the SUV he was driving due to the icy road conditions. The accident left him with debilitating spinal cord injuries that may have been prevented if he had been wearing a seatbelt. He died on February 8, 2000, due to a massive pulmonary embolism related to his injuries. His death was a tragic and unnecessary loss. It should have been left at that.

> *"The reason people blame things on the previous generation is that there's only one other choice."*
> *— Doug Larson*

Instead, his mother, Edith Morgan sued General Motors stating that her son's neck was broken because the roof of the SUV collapsed a few inches. Her lawyer begged jurors to award more than $100 million in damages... or more. The lawyer stated that he "did not want to put an upper limit on it." GM pointed out that Thomas's oversize SUV was exempt from federal roof crush standards, yet GM met them anyway. The jury did the right thing and sent a strong and rare message: of the $100 million that was requested, the jury awarded Morgan nothing.

In 1999, a 27 year old drifter in Florida trespassed on to SeaWorld property, snuck past security, scaled two clearly marked barriers, took off his clothes, and jumped into 50-degree water with an 11,000-pound killer whale. He was found dead by park security and his parents decided to sue. The lawyers alleged that the dangerous orca was portrayed as a huggable stuffed toy and the park was legally liable because it portrayed the killer whale as human-loving. Lawyers also claimed that the park should warn visitors that the animal could kill people who enter the water. I guess calling it a "killer whale" isn't good enough huh? Another tragic death, but let's face the facts—people make stupid decisions and sometimes it costs them their lives. That doesn't mean we have the right to blame someone else and sue over it!

> *"All blame is a waste of time. No matter how much fault you find with another, and regardless of how much you blame him, it will not change you."*
> *— Wayne Dyer*

A youth baseball coach in Ohio was sued by the catcher's father. The $2,000 lawsuit claimed that the incompetence of the coach cost the team a trip to a tournament in Florida. "I didn't understand it," says Carroll, 43, a street-maintenance worker who had volunteered for two years. "I wanted to be a coach just to help kids." A few words to that catcher's father: It's youth baseball dude! Lighten up! Maybe your kid just stinks at it.

A man filed a lawsuit in Atlanta against the maker of Liquid Fire drain cleaner after the stuff oozed out of his homemade container all over his legs, causing "extensive, excruciating burns and destruction of flesh." Basically, he burned himself. Liquid Fire actually comes in a spill-proof container, but the plaintiff was skeptical of its sturdiness, so he poured the contents into his own, "safer" container (the one he spilled on himself). His case claims that Liquid Fire's original package somehow created the impression of flimsiness, which therefore forced him to pour the contents into his own container. Therefore, the whole accident must have been *their* fault. What an idiot!

> *"As human beings, we are endowed with freedom of choice, and we cannot shuffle off our responsibility upon the shoulders of God or nature. We must shoulder it ourselves. It is our responsibility."*
> *— Arnold J. Toynbee*

Norman Mayo suffered a stroke because his arteries were clogged from years of chugging milk. So he decided to sue the milk industry because the containers didn't carry a warning about fat and cholesterol. "I drank milk like some people drink beer or water. I've always loved a nice cold glass of milk, and I've drank a lot of it." This guy sued the Safeway supermarket chain and the Dairy Farmers of Washington in federal court. "If tobacco products can be required to have warning labels, why not dairy products?" was Mayo's question. "I think milk is just as dangerous as tobacco. It's my opinion that the dairy industry's to blame. They push their dairy products without warning you of the hazards." People who can't be responsible for moderation in their lives just sue. Thankfully, the lawsuit was thrown out.

A couple tried to sue a health club in California. Apparently the husband had a short-lived, but serious, cyber affair with another woman. The couple was suing for loss of consortium and emotional distress blaming the health club for the internet relationship. The couple claimed that if the man hadn't cut his hand on a towel dispenser at the health club and had to spend time at home recuperating, he wouldn't have had the time to spend on the home computer roving around. Are you kidding me? I guess we'll go to any length to ***not*** take responsibility!

We need to wake up and smell the lawsuits people! We are raising up a new generation of kids who refuse to look at themselves when things go wrong. We are teaching them as a society to cast blame on others and sue anyone you can! Look folks, if you chop your toe off with a lawnmower, you are not entitled to a $50 million dollar settlement from Black and Decker for making the blade too sharp—learn to be more careful! Take responsibility people!

STUPID WARNING LABELS

So what's the result of ridiculous lawsuits? We have to make concessions for all these idiots in the world. We have to warn them about every possible thing to protect them from themselves. It's all of these stupid, ridiculous lawsuits that result in people not taking responsibility that result in stupid, ridiculous warning labels. Before you look at the ones below, keep in mind that someone actually had to have done these things and complained about them or sued over them before a company would have to spend money on a wacky warning label!

On a digital thermometer:
WARNING: Do not use orally after using rectally.
(Who's the moron who called up and admitted to ***that****?)*

On a cartridge for a laser printer:
WARNING: Do not eat toner.
(Who are these people and how hungry do you have to be?)

On an adult batman costume:
WARNING: Cape does not enable user to fly.
(Somebody's been smoking something illegal... in most states)

On a Baby stroller:
WARNING: Remove child before folding.
(If someone has to tell you that, you probably shouldn't be allowed to reproduce!)

On a Curling Iron:
WARNING: This product can burn eyes.
(Ladies, it's NOT an eyelash curler!)

On a Rowenta Iron:
WARNING: Never iron clothes on the body.
(Are we in that big of a hurry?!)

On a McDonald's Coffee Cup:
WARNING: Contents may be hot.
(We all know where that one came from!)

On a Japanese GameCube Instruction Manual:

WARNING: Do not attempt to stick head inside deck, which may result in injury.

(It's time to stop playing and get a life!)

On a Dremel Electric Rotary Tool:

WARNING: This product not intended for use as a dental drill.

(Trying to save money on the dentist?)

On a Hair Coloring Bottle:

WARNING: Do not use as an ice cream topping.

(So the bad smell didn't tip you off huh?)

On the Microsoft Flight Simulator 2000 Software:

WARNING: This program should not be used in flight training! Death or serious injury could result!

(And we wonder how terrorists got into flight school!)

On a Golf Cart:

WARNING: Not for highway use.

(I think I was driving behind the guy who tried that!)

On a shot gun:

WARNING: Do not use with Vice President Dick Cheney.

(Ok, I made that one up!)

I don't know about you, but personally, I am pretty sick of this stuff! I think it's high time we started exercising some common sense. But then again, it's just not so common anymore, is it?

8

It's Not So Common Anymore

Exercise Some Common Sense!

The American Heritage® Dictionary defines common sense as: "Sound judgment not based on specialized knowledge." So common sense does not require formal education, special training classes, or a lecture from your parent or teacher. It's something we are supposed to possess without someone else explaining it to us. Yet if you look around, what you might consider common sense is not so common anymore. To be successful, you must practice some simple common sense.

We live in a society now where we must have seminars and classes on "ethics." We have to teach people what ethical behavior looks like. Now ethical behavior is just common sense people. If someone has to tell you to say no when your boss asks you to forge an accounting document, then you're just stupid. If that statement offends you then stop being stupid. I'll stop being offensive if you stop being stupid.

We have become desensitized to what is right and wrong, but that doesn't change the fact that it's still common sense. Everyone knows the difference between right and wrong. It's etched in you whether you admit it or not. It's called a God-given conscience. I don't care if you believe in God or not. You don't have to. I don't have to believe in the wind, but if I go outside and the wind is blowing, my hair is still going to get messed up. I can choose to explain it away in any creative way I want to. After all, this is America! Freedom of speech, freedom of thought, freedom of religion, freedom of expression, freedom of stupidity—we have it all! All those freedoms still don't negate certain things that are just common sense.

> *"Common sense is the knack of seeing things as they are, and doing things as they ought to be done."*
> *—H. Beecher Stowe*

So back to the conscience issue—when you ignore your conscience enough, it becomes hardened. I have been there and that's not a place you want to get to if you can at all avoid it. The best way to avoid it is to use common sense and make the right choices.

COMMON SENSE RAMBLINGS

It's a crazy world we live in! I would now like to dedicate this section to what I call the common sense ramblings of an angry American (that's me!). These are some of the common sense issues that irk me:

- Common sense dictates that you should educate yourself about products before you use them. Manufacturers provide plenty of instruction manuals.

If you are too lazy to educate yourself and misuse the product, don't blame the company who made it—blame yourself and admit your stupidity!

➢ Common sense dictates that you should know and understand the consequences of your choices. I was recently summoned for jury duty on a civil and criminal case wrapped into one. We were being asked as a jury to decide whether or not a patient at a mental institution was still mentally ill enough to be a danger to society. I raised my hand and asked what the outcome of our decision would be. Would it determine if he was released into society or sent back to prison? We were told that we would not have the opportunity to know the consequence of our decision and did anyone have a problem with that. I was shocked to be the only one to raise my hand. "Yes, I have a very big problem with not knowing the consequence of my decision." Not surprisingly, I was dismissed as a potential juror.

> *"It is a thousand times better to have common sense without education than to have education without common sense."*
> *—R. Green Ingersoll*

➢ Common sense dictates that if you don't work hard, pay your dues, and stop making excuses, you will end up with nothing. If that's your choice, so be it. But don't expect the successful people who did work hard and pay their dues to support you.

➢ Common sense dictates that if you smoke, eat junk food, drink excessively, and don't exercise, you'll end up with health problems. You may even kill yourself. Again, it's a free country—do what you want with your health. But if you get sick, don't look for others to blame—just be honest and blame yourself! Don't look for others to pay your health bills because of your bad choices either.

- Common sense dictates that if you work in any type of retail store at the counter and a customer walks up, stop talking to your coworkers or friends. It's rude to the person who is trying to give you money. At least *act* like you appreciate their business. Smile. Ask how they're doing. Show some courtesy. If you can't do this, go work somewhere else. Chances are you won't be missed anyway (at least not by the customers!).
- Common sense dictates that you shouldn't bring pornographic materials into the workplace or make pornographic remarks. If someone has to explain this to you or make you take a class on "hostile environment" because of it, you're just stupid and shouldn't be allowed to collect a paycheck.
- Common sense dictates that you turn your cell phone off in a nice restaurant. People don't spend copious amounts of money to go out to a nice dinner so they can hear your phone ring and listen to you talk to someone like you're so stinkin' important! If your life is structured in such a way that you can't enjoy a nice evening out without someone "needing you," then you have done a pathetic job of organizing your life and empowering others. That would make you a very bad leader.

> *"Common sense is genius dressed in its working clothes."*
> *—R. Waldo Emerson*

- Common sense dictates that you don't take very young children out to nice restaurants. Children are prone to crying and outbursts in public. Many people in that restaurant paid a babysitter to get away from that very problem. They wanted a nice quiet evening out and your screaming two-year-old is ruining the ambience! That's rude and so are you if you do that.

- Common sense dictates that when you are in a meeting or a seminar, that you give the person who is speaking your full attention. This is not the time to email someone or check your messages. Put your technological gadgets down and show some courtesy.
- Common sense dictates that it's rude to blow smoke in someone's face. If you want to kill yourself smoking, that's fine. It's a free country. I like to drink organic vegetable juice. I think you'd be pretty offended if I walked up to you and spit my juice in your mouth and forced *you* to drink it. Well that's what you do when you blow smoke in my face. It's disgusting. Please stop. And don't throw those disgusting butts on the ground. There are plenty of trash receptacles. If you can't find one, put it in your pocket!
- Common sense dictates that you shouldn't put your make-up on while you drive. You shouldn't try to read the newspaper. You shouldn't try to program your new stereo. You shouldn't try to flick the screaming kids in the back seat (no matter how much they deserve it). You shouldn't try to send a text message on your cell phone. You shouldn't be rummaging around for something in the glove box. Pay attention when you drive! And watch the lights turn colors so you're not sitting there like an idiot after it turns green.
- Common sense dictates that we use manners when dealing with others. We need to stop being rude as a society.
- Common sense dictates that we need to teach our children some manners, yet it amazes me how rude so many young children and teenagers are these days. We need to be teaching our kids to say please and thank you. We need to teach them to respect adults and authority. We need to hold them

accountable. As a society, we have all but stopped spanking our children—how did that work out for us? It has resulted in an entitlement-based, rude society. If a kid needs to be spanked, then spank him. I'm not talking about child abuse. I am talking about disciplining your child out of love and having consequences for actions. I'm talking about a good swat on the bottom (again, not when angry).

If you do this when they are young, you can use the removed privileges technique when they are older. We have exhausted time outs and helping their little self-esteem. Most teens these days are full of themselves and full of self-esteem. They have the self esteem to get into the face of a teacher or their parents and let them know they can't touch them. What they need isn't more self-esteem—what they need is more time with their parents and more discipline. Common sense dictates that escalating consequences will deter future bad behavior. No one can stand to be around kids who are not disciplined. You're only hurting your kids by allowing them to turn out to be little monsters that no one can tolerate.

> *"In the war for individual rights, common sense becomes the first and major casualty."*
> *—Unknown*

I was talking with a woman one day and she was telling me how "out of control" her eight-year-old son was. She told me he throws objects in a fit of rage, slams doors, and kicks her when he's angry. I asked her what the consequences were. She said she was told to let him express himself and if it gets out of control to send him to his room. So I asked, "Yeah, and how has that worked out for you?" Her answer: "Not too well." What a shocker!

One of the reasons so many lawyers have a job is because we lack common sense. When you look at some of the stupid laws all of our states have put into place, you can begin to see where we lack common sense. Just to prove it, I'll give you one stupid law or ordinance from each state. Some of these have been left on the books for decades and decades because people are too stupid to make the changes! I could give you tons for each state, but I'll spare you and just show you one for each state:

- Alabama: It's illegal to stab yourself to gain someone's pity.
- Alaska: It is illegal to push a live moose out of a moving airplane.
- Arizona: It is illegal to hunt camels.
- Arkansas: It is illegal to keep an alligator in a bathtub.
- California: It is illegal to detonate a nuclear device within city limits.
- Colorado: It is illegal for barbers to give massages to nude customers unless it is for instructional purposes.
- Connecticut: In one city, it is illegal to play Scrabble while waiting for a politician to speak.
- Delaware: It is illegal to get married on a dare.
- Florida: It is illegal for men to be seen publicly in any kind of strapless gown.
- Georgia: In one city, it is illegal to tie a giraffe to a telephone pole or street lamp.
- Hawaii: It is illegal to get a tattoo behind your ear or on your eyelid unless a registered physician is present.

- Idaho: In one city, if you're 88 years old or older, it is illegal for you to ride your motorcycle.
- Illinois: A city ordinance makes it illegal to take a poodle to the opera.
- Indiana: A person must wait four hours after eating garlic before entering a movie house, or riding a public streetcar.
- Iowa: One-armed piano players must perform for free.
- Kansas: If two trains meet on the same track, neither shall proceed until the other has passed.
- Kentucky: It is illegal to transport an ice cream cone in your pocket.
- Louisiana: It is illegal to rob a bank and then shoot at the bank teller with a water pistol.
- Maine: It is illegal to step out of a plane while in flight.
- Maryland: It is illegal to throw a bail of hay out of a second story window.
- Massachusetts: Bullets can not be used as currency.
- Michigan: It is **legal** for a robber to file a law suit if the robber gets injured in your house.
- Minnesota: It is illegal to tease skunks.
- Mississippi: In one city, it is illegal to shave in the middle of Main Street.
- Missouri: It is illegal to sit on the curb of any city street and drink beer from a bucket.
- Montana: It is illegal to have a sheep in the cab of your truck without a chaperone.
- Nebraska: It is illegal to sneeze or burp in church.
- Nevada: It is against the law to pawn your dentures.

- New Hampshire: It is illegal to sell the clothes you are wearing to pay off a gambling debt.
- New Jersey: It is against the law to frown at a police officer.
- New Mexico: It is illegal for cab drivers to reach out and physically pull potential customers into their cabs.
- New York: It is against the law to throw a ball at someone's head for fun.
- North Carolina: It is against the law to roller blade on a state highway.
- North Dakota: Horses are prohibited from sleeping in tubs.
- Ohio: It is **legal** for a police officer to bite a dog to shut it up.
- Okalahoma: It is unlawful to put any hypnotized person in a display window.
- Oregon: It's illegal to walk down a sidewalk and knock a snake's head off with your cane.
- Pennsylvania: It is illegal to use dynamite to catch fish.
- Rhode Island: Any marriage where either of the parties is an idiot or lunatic can be deemed null and void.
- South Carolina: It is illegal to sell merchandise within a half mile of a church unless fruit is being sold.
- South Dakota: It is illegal to lie down and fall asleep in a cheese factory.
- Tennessee: It is illegal to catch a fish with a lasso.
- Texas: It is illegal to milk another person's cow.
- Utah: In one city, you must be able to see daylight between two dancing partners.
- Vermont: It is illegal to whistle underwater.

- Virginia: In one city, it is illegal to flip a coin in a restaurant to see who pays for coffee.
- Washington: It is illegal to ride an ugly horse.
- West Virginia: In one county, it is illegal for a member of the clergy to tell jokes or humorous stories from the pulpit during a church service.
- Wisconsin: It is illegal to wake a fireman when he is asleep.
- Wyoming: One city ordinance forbids couples from having sex while standing inside a store's walk-in meat freezer.

Common sense dictates that we now live in a society lacking common sense. When we have to put a warning label on a cup of coffee to tell people the contents are hot, we know we've lost most of our common sense. At least train and educate your children to have some common sense so our next generation won't perpetuate the massive epidemic of deteriorating common sense!

9

Stop Being a Baby

Face Your Fears and Take Some Risks!

Fear keeps people in their homes, stuck in jobs they hate, trapped in relationships they are too afraid to change, and stagnant in every area of their lives. Fear keeps people from taking the necessary risks to become successful. Philosopher William James once said, "If you want to change your life, you must do it immediately and flamboyantly." That requires risk and it requires facing your fears.

There is a reason why people find it difficult to face their fears or take risks in life: the terror of failure. People fear failure and yet most success stories in life are the result of overcome failures. I have failed more times in my life than I have succeeded.

Do you know why a full grown, multi-ton circus elephant can be held captive by a small pole and a light chain that is cuffed to its ankle and it won't try to escape? I asked this at a firefighter conference once and one of the guys yelled out, "Because he's married…?" No! It's not because the elephant is married! The reason the elephant won't try to escape is because the elephant was preconditioned to believe it is not strong enough to escape. When the elephant was very small, it was held by that same pole and chain and when it tried to pull on it and break free, the elephant failed. It would continue to try and fail… try and fail. After awhile, the elephant just believes it will always fail; therefore, it just stops trying. So even as a full-grown, mutli-ton animal that could yank that chain loose in one strong pull, the elephant won't even take the risk. It remains chained to its past failures.

> *"Avoiding danger is no safer in the long run than outright exposure. Life is either a daring adventure, or nothing."*
> *— Helen Keller*

Humans are the same way. If we have failed at something in the past, we precondition ourselves to believe we will fail again and so we often won't try. We won't risk failure. If we have failed a great deal, we tend to stop trying at most everything. The best success stories in life are people who have risked failure or overcome multiple failures.

BABE AND WALT

Babe Ruth was named baseball's Greatest Player Ever in 1998. He had the record for the most home runs in a season (60) in 1927 and that record wasn't broken until 1961 (by Roger Maris). Babe Ruth had 714 career home runs, which was nearly three times higher than the next highest record. He was considered baseball's biggest success story. He was the most famous person at the time of his death.

Babe Ruth was at bat 8,399 times in his career! He had to stand at that plate over 8,000 times to get those 714 home runs. He had to take a lot of risk. In the midst of risking failure, he failed quite a bit too. Babe Ruth struck out 1,330 times in his career. There are few glorious successes in life that have not had to risk failure. We have to strike out quite often to experience the glory of real success in life.

I mentioned Walt Disney in earlier chapters. I often wonder if people think he was just an overnight success story. I wonder if people realize how much he risked failure. Stephen Schochet has compiled ten major setbacks that were endured by Walt Disney in the process of becoming successful. This is a man who continued to take risks! (reprinted with permission from: http://www.disneydreamer.com)

1) Walt formed his first animation company in Kansas City in 1921. He made a deal with a distribution company in New York. Walt would ship them his cartoons and get paid six months down the road. Flushed with success, he began to experiment with some new storytelling techniques. His costs went up, and then the distributor went bankrupt. He was forced to dissolve his company, and at one point could not pay his rent and was surviving by eating dog food.

> *"Courage is the main quality of leadership, in my opinion, no matter where it is exercised. Usually it implies some risk--especially in new undertakings."*
> *—Walt Disney*

2) Walt created a mildly successful cartoon character in 1926 called Oswald the Rabbit. When he tried to negotiate with his distributor (Universal Studios) for better rates for each cartoon, he was informed that Universal had obtained ownership of the Oswald character and they had hired Disney's artists out from under him.

3) When Walt tried to get MGM studios to distribute Mickey Mouse in 1927 he was told that the idea would never work—a giant mouse on the screen would terrify women.

4) The Three Little Pigs was rejected by distributors in 1933 because it only had four characters. It was felt at that time that cartoons should have as many figures on the screen as possible. It later became very successful and played at one theater so long that the poster outside featured the pigs with long white beards.

5) Snow White and the Seven Dwarfs was sneak previewed to college students in 1937 who left halfway during the film causing Disney great despair. It turned out the students had to leave early because of dorm curfew.

6) Pinocchio in 1940 became extra expensive because Walt shut down the production to make the puppet more sympathetic than the lying juvenile delinquent as presented in the original Carlo Col-

> *"It's kind of fun to do the impossible."*
> *—Walt Disney*

lodi story. He also resurrected a minor character, an unnamed cricket who tried to tell Pinocchio the difference between right and wrong until the puppet killed him with the mallet. Excited by the development of Jiminy Cricket (plus the revamped, misguided rather than rotten Pinocchio) Walt poured extra money into the film's special effects and it ended up losing a million dollars in its first release.

7) For the premiere of Pinocchio, Walt hired eleven midgets, dressed them up like the little puppets, and then put them on top of Radio City Music Hall in New York with a full day's supply of food and wine. The idea was they would wave hello to the little children entering into the theater. By the middle of the hot afternoon, there were eleven drunken, naked midgets running around the top of the marquee, screaming obscenities at the crowd below. The most embarrassed people were the police who had to climb up ladders and take the little fellows off in pillowcases.

> *"Somehow I can't believe there are any heights that can't be scaled by a man who knows the secret of making dreams come true."*
> *—Walt Disney*

8) Walt never lived to see Fantasia become a success. The 1940 audiences were put off by its lack of a story. Also the final scene, The Night On Bald Mountain sequence with the devil damning the souls of the dead, was considered unfit for children.

9) In 1942, Walt was in attendance for the premiere of Bambi. In the dramatic scene where Bambi's mother died, Bambi was shown wandering through the meadow shouting, "Mother! Where are you, Mother?" A teenage girl seated in the balcony shouted out, "Here I am Bambi!" The audience broke into laughter except for the red-faced Walt who concluded correctly that war-time was not the best time to release a film about the love-life of a deer.

10) The sentimental Pollyanna in 1960 made Walt cry at the studio screening but failed at the box office. Walt concluded that the title was off-putting for young boys.

Walt was human. He suffered through many fits of anger and depression through his many trials. Yet he learned from each setback, and continued to take even bigger risks which led to fabulous financial rewards when combined with the wisdom that experiencing failure provided.

There are so many other setbacks, trials, and obstacles that Walt faced. He purchased a house for his parents, but it had some sort of defect in the heating unit. His mother died of carbon monoxide poisoning and his father suffered severe damage. This man's life was full of risk, failure, and triumph. Sometimes they all come in one package.

I WAS AN ELEPHANT ONCE

There was a time in my life when I was like that circus elephant I described earlier. I failed at public speaking at a very young age and I didn't want to risk failure again. I remained chained to my past failures instead of facing the fear and taking the risks that I needed to take.

The first time I was asked to speak publicly I was fourteen years old. I was asked to narrate a play. I had never been in front of a group, so I had no idea that the fear of public speaking ranked number one over the fear of death and divorce. People would rather get a divorce or ***die*** before getting up in front of people to speak. I didn't know that, so I agreed to narrate this play. I soon discovered ***why*** people would rather die.

When the curtain opened and it came time to speak, I saw 600 eyes staring at me and the public speaking terror hit me. It started at my knees and they began to knock together. Then it moved up to my stomach where it put my lunch on the spin cycle. Then it slithered up to my neck and constricted every muscle in my throat until I could barely breathe. Then it moved to my mouth and siphoned every last drop of saliva left in me until I was left sucking cotton. Then my eyes went blurry, my hands started to shake, and I opened my mouth to speak.

What eeked out of me was the most horrifying sound you've ever heard. My voice cracked and trembled with terror. I looked out at the audience and they had that pained look on their face. I could read their minds: *"This is hurting us much more than it is you!"* I failed miserably and I swore I would never get up in front of a group again. What scares me about that is this: I caught part of an episode of Fear Factor awhile back, and I swore for $50,000, I would never crunch and munch on a cow eyeball! Well considering I swore I would never get up in front of people and speak and I now do that for a living, that cow eyeball oath isn't looking too promising!

> *"The dangers of life are infinite, and among them is safety."*
> *— Goethe*

But I did manage to dodge the public speaking bullet for twelve years. I avoided speech class, I wouldn't run for school office, and I dodged anything that would require me to get up in front of people and speak. I was not about to risk failure again. It wasn't until I was twenty six years old that an event in my life pushed me to overcome this fear.

I was sitting in church one Sunday before the service started. My husband got up to go to the restroom and the pastor came by and tapped me on the shoulder. He said, "Kim, I need you to give the announcements today—someone didn't show up." Then he disappeared before I could refuse. I was filled with terror once again. My hands started to shake, my stomach started to ache, and sweat starting pouring down my sides.

My husband came back from the restroom and sat down next to me. I said, "Honey, you are not going to believe what just happened. The pastor just came by here, and wants ***you*** to give the announcements today."

> *"If you want to overcome fear, do that which you fear and keep on doing it until you have a record of successful experiences behind you. That is the surest and quickest way yet discovered to conquer fear."*
> *—Dale Carnegie*

That's when I knew I had a problem. I was willing to lie… in church! I knew it was time to get a grip on this problem. So I faced the fear and started teaching an adult community education class at our local college. It took me a good year to get comfortable with it. It took me two years to actually like it. It took me three years to realize I had a passion for it. That passion would have stayed hidden within my fear had I not risked failure and pushed through it.

Mark Twain once said, “Courage is the resistance to fear and the mastery of fear, not the absence of fear. Unless a creature be part coward, it is not a compliment to say it is brave.” Successful people are not absent of fear, they just master fear and succeed in spite of it. And they have to take risks.

I had another huge fear in my life. The fear of heights and small planes. I learned my lesson from my fear of speaking so I decided to change this area of my life. I took the advice of philosopher William James, and I did it immediately and flamboyantly. I decided to become a licensed pilot. It was one of the hardest things I ever attempted. I had to push myself daily to conquer that fear. For the first three months, every time I went up in that plane I had a panic attack and tried to hide it so my instructor wouldn’t boot me out of the program. I whined and complained and blamed it on the plane and do you know what my instructor told me? He said, “Kim, the problem is probably not the plane, it’s probably YOU! I hate it when he’s right. So every day I took a risk and I faced that fear.

It wasn’t easy either with such a sarcastic air traffic controller in the tower where I was learning to fly. When I finally learned to fly solo, without my instructor, I would go out to the airport and practice my takeoffs and landings. Every time I did, that mean air traffic controller always had something sarcastic to say. I was on final approach one morning for my practice landings when I found myself fighting some nasty, gusting wind. My right wing came down too low. I over-corrected and then my left wing came down too low. Then I brought the nose up too high, and then too low. Then I

> *"You gain strength, courage and confidence by every experience in which you really stop to look fear in the face."*
> *—Eleanor Roosevelt*

touched down on one wheel, lifted up, leveled out, and then bounced that plane all the way down the runway. I looked like a hyperactive kid on a pogo stick!

I taxied off the runway and that mean air traffic controller couldn't wait to breech the airways: "Cherokee 3477 Quebec this is San Luis Obispo tower. Did you just land or were you shot down?" I was not about to go quietly. I gave it right back to him. "San Luis tower, 3477 Quebec here. I know that landing wasn't your fault. It really wasn't my fault. It must have been the asphalt!"

I didn't let him or the fear keep me from my goal. After nine months of grueling lessons and conquering my fear, I got my pilot's license. Now I'm no Maverick from Top Gun, but I believe that any landing you can walk away from or limp away from is a good landing!

Don't be an elephant like I was. Don't remain chained to your past failures. Whatever it is you have failed at in the past... get over it! Move on! You have the strength to succeed today. Whatever it is you need to take a risk on to succeed, take the risk! All success requires risk. You have to take risks in every area of your life to be successful: your personal relationships, your kids, your work, your life is one big risk! So take the risk and live life to the fullest. If you're not living on the edge, then you're missing some of the best views the good Lord has to offer. So stop being a baby, take the risk, and face your fears!

> *"Progress always involves risk; you can't steal second base and keep your foot on first."*
> *— Frederick Wilcox*

10

Stop Being Annoying

The Four Types of Annoying People

Yes, You're One of Them!

I know most people think of others as being annoying and not themselves, but if everyone thinks everyone else is annoying, then everyone is pretty much annoying. You can be who you are without making people want to rip off their own arm just so they have something to beat you over the head with! There are four types of annoying people in the world, and I can guarantee you—you're one of them!

THE ANALYTICAL

The first type of annoying person is the Analytical. They are introverted in nature and are very task-oriented people. They are the brainiacs in the world! Engineers, computer programmers, number crunchers, and rocket scientists are all Analyticals. They love numbers, graphs, charts and statistics. The Analyticals are organized, systematic, and exact. They would rather make no decision than a bad decision. They want things done right the first time.

So why are they so annoying? They can be moody, critical, and negative. They can also be too serious, unsociable, and indecisive. They are extremely over-analyzing in nature and provide way too much information. If they're telling you a story, it goes something like this: "I was pulling up the application for a process management evaluation on Tuesday at 10:00 am… oh wait, maybe it was 9:56 am because that's when the electricity surged, my digital clock flickered, the motherboard crashed, my hard drive went down and I lost all of my data." And everyone around them is thinking, "WHO CARES?! Get to the point!"

If you're an Analytical, you over-analyze everything. Three golfers went out one day to play a round of golf. One was a doctor, one was a pastor, and one was an Analytical. As they progressed to the second hole, they noticed a foursome in front of them moving slower than a snail. This went on for several holes until they all starting getting frustrated. The doctor said, "This is ridiculous, they are so slow!" The Analytical said, "You're right! I have never seen such ineptitude." The pastor said, "Yes, this is a little frustrating."

> *"I told my psychiatrist that everyone hates me. He said I was being ridiculous - everyone hasn't met me yet."*
> *—Rodney Dangerfield*

Just about then the greens keeper drove by on his golf cart and they waived him down. The pastor said,

"George, could you help us out? The foursome in front of us is moving rather slowly today."

George peered down the fairway and then sighed heavily. He looked sympathetically at the golfers and said, "Yeah, those guys are firefighters. They lost their eyesight saving our clubhouse last year, so we let them play golf for free anytime they want to."

The pastor felt horrible. "Oh that is just so sad. I will go home tonight and say a prayer for them." The doctor jumped right in. "Yes, and I will call my ophthalmologist friend and see if there is anything he can do to help." They all turned to look at the Analytical. He was thinking intently. He finally said, "I just don't understand why these guys can't play at night!"

> *"I like long walks, especially when they are taken by people who annoy me."*
> *—Noel Coward*

That's just the way they think. An optimist says the glass is half full. A pessimist says the glass is half empty. An Analytical says the glass is twice as big as it needs to be.

If you're an Analytical, there are some things you can do to be less annoying. First of all, you can make a decision. Once you have all of the facts and data, stop dragging your feet and take some action! The next thing you can do is lighten up on the perfectionist issue. You tend to have high expectations of everyone around you. Get out and socialize more, step away from the computer, and interact with people!

THE DRIVER

The second type of annoying person is the Driver: They are also task-oriented like the Analytical, but they are extroverted in nature. Drivers are Type A, driven, natural-born leaders. They would rather make a bad decision than no decision—they just want the decision to be made!

What makes them so annoying? They can be insensitive, harsh, proud, and sarcastic. The word sarcasm comes from the root word *sarkasmose* which means to rip and tear at the flesh like dogs. And the Drivers reading this are thinking "She's saying that like it's a *bad* thing, right?" Drivers are the kings and queens of sarcasm.

Drivers are the ones who came up with the mean, sarcastic animal phrases, mostly about cats, and tried to subtly integrate them into society as clichés. You use them every day. Like, "There's more than one way to skin a cat." Only a Driver would actually know that! Or, "Curiosity killed the cat." Or, "Who let the cat out of the bag?" I think the better question is "Who put the cat in the bag?" A Driver I think! Well as a Driver (yes, I confess, I have a lot of the Driver annoying type in me), I have come up with a new sarcastic cat phrase that I plan to infiltrate into society. "A cat in the toilet is better than two on the couch!"

> *"Don't walk in front of me, I may not follow; Don't walk behind me, I may not lead; Don't walk beside me either. Just leave me alone."*

Drivers are also annoying because they tend to put work or tasks before everything else in life. They are known for being "workaholics," and they rarely take time to relax and sit still. They tend to be controlling in nature and roll over the top of people. They are often accused of being a bull in a china shop. They are huge initiators and get a lot of stuff done. However, they don't always think through the details. As a result, they get stuff done quickly, but not always correctly. If you want to get to the moon, hire a Driver. If you want to get back, hire an Analytical!

Drivers could be less annoying if they would curb their sarcasm. They also need to exercise patience with incompetence and show some compassion. Drivers often come off as know-it-alls, so they could be less annoying if they stopped correcting everyone. Drivers are very intense, competitive, and productive people. They need to think more about relationships and less about work to find the balance in life. If you're a Driver, show concern for people!

THE AMIABLE

The third type of annoying person is the Amiable. They are introverted in nature like the Analytical, but they are relationship oriented, not task oriented. Amiables like people and they like to please others. They are the sweetest, kindest, nicest, easy going people on the face of the earth. Makes you want to puke!

So what's so annoying about them? First of all, they avoid conflict at all costs. I was in the grocery store a few months ago, and I can guarantee you the guy in the aisle next to me was an Amiable. He was pushing his cart through the store and he had a four year old boy in the front of the cart who was throwing a fit. He was arching his back and screaming, "Daaaaad, I want some candy!" The dad just kept pushing the cart saying, "It's ok Donny. Just stay calm. We're going to be out of here in five minutes."

> *"I am free of all prejudices. I hate everyone equally."*
> *— W.C. Fields*

This kid was not phased "NOOOOOOO! I want it now! Give me that candy!" The dad just kept talking in a soothing voice. "Don't freak out Donny. Just two more minutes and we'll be going home to take a nice long nap. Just stay calm Donny."

I couldn't help myself. I went up to the guy and said, "WOW! You are the most patient dad I have ever seen.

You've got a real handful here with little Donny." He said, "No, no... my son's name is Michael. *I'm* Donny." Typical Amiable, get some backbone people and deal with conflict!

Amiables are the type of people who don't like to make decisions. They just say, "I don't care—what do you want to do?" They just want to keep the peace in life and their focus is more on relationships than work or tasks that need to be accomplished.

> *"Only the wisest and stupidest of men never change."*
> *—Confucius*

If you're an Amaible, you could be less annoying by speaking up and really saying what is on your mind. Stop placating people and deal with conflict. You could also be on time and not be so blasé about things. To have a little more balance in life, concentrate on some of the tasks that need to be done and not always just on relationships.

THE EXPRESSIVE

The last and loudest type of annoying person is the Expressive. They are the party animals. If you ever go to a party and see someone standing on the table with a lamp shade on their head—that's an Expressive! They are charismatic, fun-loving, cheerful people who enter the room mouth first. They can talk up to 200 words per minute with gusts up to 300.

My adult son is an Expressive. When he was little, the teacher sent home his report card with a note attached to it. The note said, "Joshua is a very intelligent little boy, but he talks way too much in class. I would like to try a new technique with him to see if I can break him of it. His father wrote a note back to the teacher. "That's a wonderful idea! Let me know if your technique works at school—I would like to try it at home... on his mother." Yes, I have a lot of Expressive with my Driver!

So what is most annoying about Expressives? First of all they are the most impatient people on the face of the earth! They are the ones who sit at their computer waiting for the browser to load, tapping their foot saying, "Come on, come on, come on! I don't have all SECOND!"

They're also annoying because they rarely think before they act and tend to make rash decisions. As I said, my son is an Expressive. When he was sixteen, we were coming back from the lake with a group of his friends. I was pulling our boat behind our SUV when the boat trailer got a flat tire. I pulled over to the side of the road and called AAA. They don't do boat trailers. So I called my husband who was about six miles away. He said he would be there in about ten minutes.

My son decided to go wait with his friends on the back of the boat trailer. I stayed in the front of the SUV playing with my cell phone. About ten minutes later, I saw the headlights pull in behind us. I got out of the car and started heading for the back of the trailer. My son was coming towards me at top speed. As he passed me he was saying "Oh crap! This is *not* happening! Oh crap!" Apparently, my son had decided to pull down his pants and flash his bare butt to my husband when he pulled up. There was just one very big problem: it wasn't my husband who pulled in behind me. It was the highway patrol! My son locked himself in the front of the SUV and I had a lot of explaining to do! Yes, my son had been in an argument with my husband earlier that day, but that is *not* what I had in mind when I advised my son to just turn the other cheek! Expressives are wild and need to think before they act!

> *"Be not angry that you cannot make others as you wish them to be, since you cannot make yourself as you wish to be."*
> *—Thomas a Kempis*

Expressives could be less annoying if they didn't always give their opinion. They could also stand to improve their listening skills and stop interrupting people when they're talking. Expressives also tend to exaggerate stories, feelings, events, etc. They will be less annoying to others if they tone down the exaggerations. Expressives are a little overwhelming to people, so lowering the voice and being less demonstrative would help too.

> *"The most important single ingredient in the formula of success is knowing how to get along with people."*
> *—Theodore Roosevelt*

So there you have it—the four types of annoying people in the world, and as you can see, you are one of them. This is a subject I like to talk about so much that I coauthored a book on the very subject called ***How to Deal With Annoying People*** (with Bob Phillips, Ph.D.). If you want to read even more about yourself and others and why you get on each other's nerves, this would be a good book to read.

If you want to be more successful in life, you need to be less annoying!

11

You're NOT as Good as it Gets!

Invest in Your Constant Improvement

If you want to be successful, you have to be in a constant state of improvement and a perpetual state of education. I am not referring to formal education, although that is certainly valuable. However, I have seen far too many people with college degrees who are not successful.

I have also seen many successful people who never even graduated high school or college. Successful people never stop learning. They have a constant hunger for new knowledge and information, and they find a way to obtain it. Whether it's books, tapes, CDs the Internet, mentors, or other successful people, successful people keep learning. But it doesn't stop there. Successful people don't just learn new information—they apply it!

YOU ARE EITHER GROWING OR DYING

If you are not constantly improving towards success in every area of your life, you are gravitating towards failure. I ran into a guy I went to high school with. He lived in the same town his entire life. He had the same views he had in high school. He had the same cap on his head. He had the same friends. He ate the same junk food. He had the same job! He had the same address (his parent's house). This guy was forty years old and never saw the need to change anything. His life is on the fast track to pathetic city! Sadly, he's not alone. There are plenty of people who live like that and figure they "just can't get a break." Well until they make a break in the cycle of deterioration, they will never "get a break."

> *"There is only one corner of the universe you can be certain of improving, and that's your own self."*
> *—Aldous Huxley*

You have to be constantly changing and improving to be successful. I have to update my laptop computer more often than I would prefer. I have to update software and programs as technology changes and develops. If I tried to use the same computer and operating system I used five years ago, not only would the system move at a snail's pace, most of the programs wouldn't be compatible with current technology and software. I would be functioning at a very low level in my business.

If you try to live your life on the same system you used five years ago without improving it in any way, you're going to find yourself functioning at a very low level. To be successful in any area of your life requires that you move forward and adapt positive changes. You have to try new things and always go for the better, stronger, and higher quality way of doing things. Whether you're talking about marriage, parenting, friendships, jobs, health, or fitness, this principle of success is not negotiable. You're either improving or you're deteriorating.

If you had a kid in the fifth grade who looked like they might not pass to the sixth grade, you would probably do everything within your power to get him/her the help needed to move on. You would study late with your child. You would employ a tutor, summer school, whatever it took. You wouldn't let your child stay in the fifth grade for ten years! Yet people will stay stuck in the same "grade" at work or at home for ten years because they are too lazy to study, get a tutor (mentor), go to summer school (seminars), or read whatever books would be needed to improve and move on. It's pathetic!

> *"Self-improvement is the name of the game, and your primary objective is to strengthen yourself, not to destroy an opponent."*
> *—Maxwell Maltz*

I grew up in poverty and no one in my family was educated. I could have stayed that way. But I knew from a very young age that I lived in the land of opportunity. No one was going to tell me I couldn't make it. I didn't expect the government to educate me. I didn't expect my neighbor to educate me. I took responsibility to educate myself. As a result, I was the first family member to graduate from high school. I was the first and only to obtain a bachelors and masters degree. When the opportunities were not available to me, I created some!

Too many people would rather stay stuck in the same job they hate, in the same position, at the same pay, with the same schedule before they will put out the effort to improve themselves. Too many people are willing to settle for mediocre relationships instead of putting out the effort to improve those relationships. Too many people are willing to accept scraping by instead of learning how to improve. There is a wealth of information out there and it's not that difficult to come by. But there is one catch: you *do* have to get off your lazy butt and get it!

IMPROVE YOUR GENERAL KNOWLEDGE

Read every day. I put my nose in a book for at least one hour every day. I don't read romance novels and I don't read horror stories. I read things that will nourish and improve me spiritually, physically, mentally, emotionally, and financially.

If you just spent fifteen minutes a day reading, you would improve your knowledge tremendously. Remember from chapter 2 that people spend an average of four hours a day watching television, or ten years of their life by the time they are 70! Even if you don't watch *that* much television, I think you would be surprised at how much you *do* watch if you started adding up all times during the week and the weekend. Make one minor change and make it today. The fact that you're reading this books shows you value improvement (or maybe it just shows you value someone who's blunt and to the point!). Take some time away from the television and commit it to some good books on ways you can improve.

> *"We are what we repeatedly do, excellence then is not an act, but a habit."*
> *— Aristotle*

Look at all of the areas of your life and see what needs improving the most. If that's your marriage, start there. If it's your relationship with your kids, start there. If it's your finances, start reading about money management. If the area that needs improving is your health and fitness, put your nose in a book that will educate you, motivate you, and inspire you (and preferably one that will kick you in the butt!).

I will say this again... reading any books will be a complete waste of time if you don't take some form of action on the information you gain. Even if you just changed one thing in your life, it would be more than worth the time you spent reading that book. Most importantly, work towards improving all areas of your life so one area does not become imbalanced.

FOCUS ON LIFE BALANCE

If you'll notice, I have listed several areas above to start improving yourself. I see so many people who are extremely successful in business, but their family life is suffering. They read books on how to be a better leader, how to adapt to change, how to embrace the management theories of the new millennium, and every best selling book on the subject of business success. All the while, they go home at 8:00 pm at night and cannot communicate with their spouse or teenagers.

I have seen people who have amazing marriages and relate to one another beautifully. They read books on the topic, go to retreats, and invest a tremendous amount of time to ensure the security of that relationship. All the while, they are letting their physical health slide as they gain more and more weight each year, struggle with health problems, and suffer from poor overall nutrition.

It seems we wrestle with attempting to be successful in all areas of our lives. If we are going to be physically healthy and vibrant, we think that we won't have enough time for work, so we'll be poor. If we are

> *"How wonderful it is that nobody need wait a single moment before starting to improve the world."*
> *—Anne Frank*

going to be financially successful, we think that we have to work long hours and we don't have time to take care of our physical bodies or develop our spiritual growth. Well I can tell you that it is possible to have balance in your life so you can be successful in all areas. In fact, it's the balance you create in your life that will bring the success across the board.

Balance home with work with play with hobbies, etc. Take vacations and have fun! Taking a vacation with the whole family can be pretty stressful, so be sure you have relaxation time at home. Most people come back from family vacations more stressed out than when they left! How often do you just sit in a quiet place and relax or think or read? Give yourself and your body a rest frequently to create more balance in your life.

START WITHIN

To be truly successful, you have to become a better person. You have to be better at relationships, work, decisions, and everything you do in life. Once you become better at everything, you have more skill and assets you can share with others. Everything improves when you improve. Your job improves when you improve. Your children, your spouse, your friends, your outlook on life, your relationships… everything—it all improves when you improve. If you want a better child, be a better parent. If you want a better parent, be a better child. If you want a better boss, be a better employee. If you want a better employee, be a better boss. If you want a better husband, be a better wife. If you want a better wife, be a better husband. You get the picture.

> *"A man can never hope to be more than he is if he is not first honest about what he isn't."*
> *—Don Williams, Jr.*

Instead of looking at what's wrong with your job, your spouse, your kids, or your friends, figure out what's wrong with you. If you need help figuring out what's wrong with you, ask your closest family and friends. I'm sure they can come up with a nice long list for you! Most people are too afraid to self-evaluate because it comes with a certain level of accountability to change what needs to be changed.

If you want your life to get better, you need to start within. Take a good long look at who you are. Where do you get your identity? What is your spiritual life like? If you are a person of faith, how much time do you invest in nourishing and developing that faith? How much time do you spend in self-evaluation asking yourself where you need to improve? Starting with yourself will exponentially improve every area of your life!

IMPROVE YOUR RELATIONSHIPS

This is definitely the area I have screwed up most in my own life in the past, so I think I can say with great confidence, you had better pay attention to this area of your life! You need to learn from the mistakes and failures of others. Let's say you're getting ready to walk down a dark alley. Just as you start to enter the alley you come face-to-face with a man who looks scared and beat up. He grabs you by the shirt and screams, "Don't go down there man! I just had a gun put to my head and I was robbed!"

Would you push him away and say "I'm not going to listen to you tell me how to not get robbed when you've been robbed! You're a failure!" Do you tell people "I'm not going to listen to you tell me how to succeed in that area when you've failed" or "I'm not going to listen to you tell me how to not get divorced—you've been divorced?" Well that's exactly why you *should* listen to people who have failed in certain areas, ***especially*** if they have figured out how to turn their lives around and succeed! Let others serve as a good warning to you in life.

I have made a lot of mistakes in my life. I have often wondered if the only purpose of my life was to serve as a warning to others! As I get older, I try to learn from those mistakes and let others learn from them too. I have often found myself grabbing someone's shirt and yelling, "Hey! Don't go down that alley! You're going to get beat up!" Some people listen and don't take the same path I took that led to failure. Others push me aside and want to see for themselves. When they come out the other side beat up and robbed, I try to contain myself and not say, "I told you so. You should have listened to my warning. You're stupid."

When you don't learn from your mistakes or the mistakes of others, you're just being stupid. I know because I've done that! I would guess that about one out of every three people is stupid (not ignorant, just stupid). Look on both sides of you… if it's not them, it's YOU!

Ok, so back to improving relationships. Don't neglect your family just to make money. Make your spouse and children a priority and a focus in your life. Invest the time it takes to have those good relationships. It's a lot of work, and it's worth the time.

We all make mistakes along the way. Some of those mistakes are bigger than others. No matter how big or small the mistake, one of the first ways you can improve relationships is to admit you made a mistake and ask forgiveness. I'm not talking about the obligatory "Look, I'm sorry, ok…?" I'm talking about "Listen. I know I messed up. I was being selfish and rude. I want to ask for your forgiveness."

> *"Learning without thought is labor lost; thought without learning is perilous."*
> *—Confucius*

The next most important area of improving relationships is to forgive and move on. Don't harbor resentment. When you continue to resent others, you allow them to live in your head rent free (I read that quote somewhere, but I don't remember who said it). True forgiveness means never bringing up the offense again—not to yourself, not to the offender, and not to others. Most people never truly forgive.

If someone has hurt you or you have experienced a loss, grieve it. Allow yourself to fully grieve that loss. But once you do, let it go. Don't live in the past and don't dwell on your losses, hurts, and disappointments. There will be plenty more in your life to deal with, and if you stay stuck on the ones in the past, you will be ill-equipped to handle the ones in the future. Allow yourself to forgive and let go.

IMPROVE YOUR HEALTH

This is such an important area! Part of true success is being healthy and taking good care of yourself. If you don't take care of your body inside and out you will experience an array of problems from headaches, stress, depression, anxiety, high blood pressure, and disease, to back pain, irritability, fatigue, digestion problems, and death (that last one is a pretty big issue!). Too many people focus on just the outside and neglect overall health. They will shove diet foods down their throat to look better on the outside while the chemicals and toxins slowly poison them on the inside. Here are just a few tips for successfully improving your health:

1. Eat better foods. The amount of junk the average American puts in their body is just insane! Just for starters, the average American eats over 150 pounds of sugar a year; over 50 gallons of soda; 27 gallons of coffee; 185 pounds of meat, poultry, and seafood; 70 pounds of butter and cooking oils, and 75 pounds of added fat just from food processing! Yep, that's right—that's just a few of the items the average American eats! And then we wonder why we have all the health problems we have and we're getting fatter by the day. We need to eat more natural and organic foods. These foods provide the life energy you need to be healthy and think clearly.

2. Drink fresh juice. This is an amazing way to get and stay healthy! The quality of our foods and soil make it impossible to get all of the nutrients we really need to be as healthy as we should be. Buy a juicer and juice organic fruits and vegetables every day. You will be amazed at how good you look and feel! Your energy level will increase and many of your health problems may disappear.

3. Exercise. The average American spends way too much time sitting on an ever-widening behind! Make the time to be more active. Take walks, go for a bike ride, get outdoors more, whatever it takes. If you ate healthy and exercised every day, you wouldn't have to go on all of those ridiculous, unhealthy fad diets. Take responsibility for your health and get active!

4. Get the rest you need. You should be getting a good night of sleep. In addition to that, if you have a stressful job (which includes taking care of kids!), you need to be finding time in the day to rest for about fifteen minutes. Just sit quietly and breathe deeply and clear your mind. Tell everyone to leave you the heck alone for fifteen minutes!

5. Laugh a lot! Laughter is one of the best medicines for good health! This is such an important area in my opinion, that I dedicated an entire chapter to having a sense of humor and loving what you do in life. It's the last chapter, so you'll just have to wait until you get there!

We are never as good as we could be. We always have room for improvement. I don't care how young or old, educated or uneducated you are—there is always room to be better. You are not as good as it gets, so get busy getting improved!

12

Find a Mentor

You Can't Do It Alone!

It's important to have role models in life. Take a look around. Slim pickings, wouldn't you say? I guess it depends on where you look for your role models. Our youth today primarily look to music performers, movie stars, and sports athletes for role models. It seems that most of these people don't care that others may look to them as role model examples. You know we live in a pathetic world when young girls are looking to Paris Hilton and Nichole Ritchie to see what they are doing with their lives, what they are wearing, who they are dating, and what night clubs they are visiting. Never mind that neither one of them is doing anything of any significance with their lives. When interviewed, Nichole Ritchie said something along the lines (and I am "para-quoting"—yes I made that word up): "People think we are spoiled, wild, and crazy... doing whatever we want. We don't care, because we are!" Christina Aguilera was actually quoted as saying "I consider myself to be a great role model…." This is someone who acts raunchy on the stage, dresses nearly naked, sings sexually suggestive songs, and all but has sex on stage. Just the kind of person every mother dreams her daughter will act like. Beautiful.

Let's not leave out the athletes. I could dedicate an entire book to this subject, but I'll just pick on one bad boy who is known as a basketball icon, but gives a bad name to the concept of role models: Dennis Rodman. Need I say more?

THE TRUMP FACTOR

Let's not leave out business icons. Donald Trump has become one of the most famous businessmen on the face of the earth. His "Apprentice" show has brought him even more notoriety. People are lined up to get on his show and become one of his employees. An apprentice is supposed to be someone who trains and learns under an expert in a particular vocation. Donald Trump is supposed to be the expert in success and business. Many people do consider him a role model and hero for business success. How can people overlook his lack of integrity? On one of his episodes, one of the teams had reserved megaphones for their assignment. The other team made the unethical move of sneaking into the store, lying about who they were, and snatching the megaphones out from under the opposing team. The unethical team won the task and avoided the boardroom. Back at the boardroom when the losing team brought up the act of dishonesty by the competing team, Trump actually praised the dishonest act! He sent the message that the end justifies the means, no

> *"Trump's philosophy is that 'unapologetic materialism is its own reward.'"*
> *—Ray Richmond*

matter how low or dirty you get. Makes you wonder how he got where he is today.

In another episode, the two teams did a good job on the task of writing a jingle, but one team had to be selected as a winner. The losing team didn't do a bad job, and there were no major errors in judgment made (other than unknowingly showing up late for the initial meeting with the executives). So the team leader had to bring two people into the boardroom with him and someone had to be fired. The team leader stuck by his guns, insisting that no one made a big enough mistake to warrant him suggesting they be fired. Keep in mind that in past episodes, Trump has gone outside the box and fired multiple people when the show only calls for one firing per episode. Trump could have gone outside the box again and surprised the world by showing some integrity and not firing anyone on this task. Instead, he tried to pigeon hole this guy and get him to turn on a teammate. When the guy insisted he wouldn't "throw anyone under the bus" just to save his own skin, Trump insisted he was left with no other choice but to fire the team leader, so he did. Trump fired him! Here was one of the few people on the show with real integrity, and Trump just didn't know what to do with it—how sad is that? But here is a man with high ratings for one of the top shows in the nation. What's happening to our role models? Why would anyone want to work for someone like that? It's just crazy!

> *"If you subscribe to the motto 'He who dies with the most toys wins', Donald Trump is ready to die a winner."*
> *—Radio Talk Show Host Adam McManus*

This is becoming more and more prevalent in society. Whatever gets good ratings and makes the money—that's what we need to do. "Whatever it takes to improve the bottom line—just do it." Well as I said earlier, what does it benefit a man to gain the whole world if he loses his soul? We need better role models than this. Success is not defined by what you get, but by what you become.

FIND A REAL ROLE MODEL

The truth is, we all really do need role models in our lives, no matter how young or old we are. We are all in a constant state of influence. We are either influencing others or being influenced by others. Without a heightened awareness that this is happening all day long, we simply allow negative influences to direct us and we often influence others negatively. You had better be very aware of whom and what is influencing you and how you are influencing others.

The best role models are usually people that have lived lives that you want to emulate. I'm not just talking about wealth and fame. I'm talking about modeling after people who have lived every area of their lives in a way you would be proud to live yours. There are few people that can live up to that kind of role model. I know I couldn't, but I will give you an example of someone who can... later in the chapter.

> *"Some people give time, some money, some their skills and connections, some literally give their life's blood. But everyone has something to give."*
> *—Barbara Bush*

Many great role models are directly involved in your life. If you can't find any, you seriously need to widen your sphere of influence. If all of your friends were made at the local whiskey bar at two in the afternoon, you might want to reconsider your lifestyle. Most people can find *some* people in their lives that they can look up to; people who experience success in many areas of their lives without compromising values, ethics, and beliefs. Maybe that person is a friend. Maybe that person is a parent or a teacher. Maybe that person is found at work or at church. They are out there and they are a vital part of modeling success.

It's great to read about successful people and how they did it, but it's also important to have people in your life who did it and continue to live it. These are the people who can hold you accountable to live the life you were called to live and not make excuses. These are the people who will kick you in the butt when you need it and tell you the things you don't always want to hear. These are the people who will tell you the truth. These people are mentors, coaches, and role models. They may not even realize they are, but they are.

I have a couple of people like this in my life—one in particular. She has been a friend since we were both pregnant together in 1984. She has been a lifelong friend who told me the truth when I didn't want to hear it. She cared enough about me to mentor me in areas where I needed it. She was honest enough to admit the mistakes in her own life. She was loyal enough to stand by my side when I made mistakes and try to direct me to the right path. She has been a mentor, a coach, and a friend. She was a role model to me as a mother. She raised her kids with fair discipline, lots of love, and plenty of consistency. She has been a role model to me as a wife. She has been married to one man since college and is committed for life. She has admitted her faults in her marriage and sought to be a better wife every day.

> *"Life, like a mirror, never gives back more than we put into it."*
> *—Anonymous*

She is a role model to me as a friend—someone who is there for other people; someone you can count on; someone you can trust; someone who would get back to you when they said they would. I wanted to be a friend like that. She is a role model to me in her work. She gives 100% to what she is doing. She has a strong work ethic. She won't compromise her values to appease others at work. She does work that she feels called to do and strives to fulfill a purpose in life, not just a space. She has been a role model to me in her faith. She lays her life down before God and strives to be in His will every day. She seeks to be better today than yesterday. Every one needs a "Rhonda" in their life.

Look around your own life for someone you admire and appreciate. Become a student of what successful people do. Find people in your life with similar talents and skills that you posses and who you admire for the success in their lives. Then find out what they did to become successful. If you know someone who you consider to be one of the best dads and very successful at parenting, mentor along side this person and glean all of the information and life experiences you can get. If you know someone who is a business genius and has been successful at starting a business and that's something you want to do, mentor with that person. Never be too prideful to learn from others.

THE BEST ROLE MODEL OF ALL TIME

When I think of the ultimate successful person on the face of the earth, I go back to my original definition of success: ***"Using your God-given gifts and talents to fulfill your God-given purpose in life."*** I think of someone who has centered his entire existence around this concept. I think of someone who was the perfect role model example in every area of life. I think of Jesus Christ. This is someone I want to role model my life after.

Jesus used his God-given gifts and talents to fulfill his God-given purpose. If you asked many people what they thought the purpose of Jesus was, most would say to teach love and forgiveness. While he was gifted in teaching those concepts, that was not his purpose. His purpose was to reconcile man with God and bring redemption. His entire life was centered around this concept, and as difficult as it was, he fulfilled his purpose with passion unto his death.

When you look at successful leaders throughout history, you tend to look at the number of followers someone had and the amount of influence the person possessed, especially years after they are gone. Jesus is the only leader in history that had so much influence on society that he split time in half (BC and AD). He has had more followers throughout history than any other leader. Even 2000 years after his death, he continues to influence society like no other leader ever has. If you want to role model your life after the most successful man in history, here are some things to model:

> *"You cannot be a leader, and ask other people to follow you, unless you know how to follow, too."*
> *—Sam Rayburn*

1. Being a servant leader. You are a leader in many areas of your life whether you recognize it or not. If you're a parent, you're a leader. If you're a friend, you're a leader. If you're a boss, you're a leader. If you want to be a successful leader, you need to learn to be a servant to others and not self-serving. Jesus had his disciples around him most of the time and these men really looked up to him. They called him "master," "teacher," and "Lord." Yet Jesus pulled out a wash basin and began to wash their feet. The disciples protested but Jesus insisted. He was trying to teach them a lesson in leading by example. To be a role model to others, you need to serve. To be successful in any area of your life you need to put others before yourself. It may shock you to discover that the world doesn't revolve around you and there are other people on this planet!

2. *Forgiveness.* Jesus was the best role model of forgiveness there is. He was an innocent man being crucified (literally), and was ready to die. Most people would scream out in anger or curse the people below them who were responsible for the unjust act, and yet Jesus extended forgiveness even in that moment. "Father, forgive them for they know not what they do." WOW! There's a role model for forgiveness. People make mistakes. Sometimes they are small and sometimes they are enormous. Forgiveness frees you from the bitterness and anger that will eat you up. Unforgiveness is a huge stumbling block to success in many areas of your life.

> *"The weak can never forgive. Forgiveness is the attribute of the strong."*
> *— Mahatma Gandhi*

3. *Stay Focused and Committed.* Jesus knew his purpose and what had to be done. He stayed focused on his mission, vision, and purpose. He stayed committed and didn't take the easy way out when he could have. Many people give up on areas of their lives when it becomes too hard, demanding, or challenging. Keeping focus and commitment can mean the difference between success and failure.

4. *Be Self-Disciplined.* No one had to follow Jesus around and tell him to do what he was made to do. He didn't have to listen to a motivational tape to pump him up. He knew what needed to be done in order for him to be successful in fulfilling his purpose, and he did it. He didn't whine or make excuses or become a victim.

5. *Don't Worry About what Other People Think.* Those closest to Jesus couldn't understand why he

didn't take his kingdom by force. They didn't understand why he didn't use his gifts, talents, and success to gain earthly position and wealth. Jesus had a different agenda for his success and he didn't care about what others thought of that. Many thought he was weird and crazy and some even accused him of being demon possessed. Jesus didn't go off and sulk about the opinions of others, nor did he let those opinions deter him from his purpose and mission in life. You have a purpose and a mission in life. Don't worry about what other people think. You are the only one who can know what true success means and what true success looks like in every area of your life.

> *"It is a privilege to serve people, a privilege that must be earned, and once earned, there is an obligation to do something good with it."*
> *—Jordan, Barbara*

We all need positive role models in our lives. Get away from the television and media, and find some truly authentic role models you can follow. Find some people in your life that can journey with you to help you find the path to success in every area of your life. Don't make excuses, just get off your butt and do it!

13

Pull the Stick Out!

Lighten Up and Laugh a Little

"If we couldn't laugh, we would all go insane!"
—Jimmy Buffet

If we couldn't laugh, we all probably ***would*** go insane! Life is dang funny and you had better learn to laugh at yourself, because you can bet other people sure will. I think people who don't have a sense of humor should not be allowed to leave their houses. They're just ruining it for the rest of us! We have to learn to lighten up and laugh a little, especially at ourselves.

You also have to love what you do and have fun at it! I woke up one day after owning a financial planning firm for ten years and realized I hated number crunching. I'm not an Analytical—I'm a Driver with a lot of

Expressive. So I took a risk and I sold my financial planning practice and pursued my passion and God-given purpose in writing and public speaking. And I love it. I have fun with it. That's how it should be. If you can't have fun at what you do, then you need to find something else to do! You don't have to love every aspect of your job, but you should at least love the type of work you do. If you don't, you have not found your passion and purpose in life.

People love to be around people who have fun at what they do. People want to do business with people who love their job and have a sense of humor. In fact, if you want to improve customer service in your organization, the quickest and surest way to accomplish that goal is to show the public that you love what you do. If you love what you do, you want to help people more… you want to solve problems… you want to make things better… you want to do a better job. If you can't find a way to show the public you love what you do, then you need to do yourself, the public, and everyone around you a favor and quit! Stop whining about how bad things are and move on. Stop making excuses about why you have to stay, and go find something you like. If you really think you're that irreplaceable, put your finger in a glass of water, pull it out, and then see how fast the hole fills in.

> *"Men will confess to treason, murder, arson, false teeth, or a wig. How many of them will own up to a lack of humor?"*
> *— Frank Moore Colby*

If everyone had a better sense of humor, the world would be a much better place! Do you know the best source of humor (besides yourself) in your life? Kids. If you don't have any, borrow someone's. Or you could check the purposefully left behind items on an airplane. I stayed at a friend's house recently and she had a little seven year old boy. We were sitting at her table in the early morning when her son emerged with a cup of coffee for his mom. It looked cold, dark, and disgusting! She looked as surprised as I did as she took the cup from him and thanked him. He said, “Go ahead mom, drink it.” She took a sip and gagged it down.

“Thanks honey.” She smiled painfully at him.

“No, Mom... drink it all. I made it special for you.” He smiled back. She winced and continued to drink it while he watched, so proud of himself. As she got about half way down the cup, she noticed some of his little green army men at the bottom. She forced a smile and asked, “Son, what are these little guys doing in here?”

He was bursting with excitement and pride! “That’s what’s special Mom! You know, just like the TV says: ‘The best part of waking up is soldiers in your cup!’ And Mom, I had to pull ‘em out of the dog’s mouth—he was chewin’ on ‘em... silly dog!”

Kids are a fantastic source of crazy humor and good clean fun. They bring lightheartedness to the table because they always say and do the funniest things! I could fill an entire book just on the funny things my own kids have said and done growing up. But instead, I’ll share this with you: A group of four to eight year olds were asked, "What does love mean?" Some of my favorite responses were:

"Love is when you tell a guy you like his shirt, then he wears it everyday." Noelle, age 7

"Love is when Mommy sees Daddy smelly and sweaty and still says he is handsomer than Brad Pitt." Chris, age 7

"Love is when your puppy licks your face even after you left him alone all day." Mary Ann, age 4

"Love is when Mommy sees Daddy on the toilet and she doesn't think it's gross." Mark, age 6

"When my grandmother got arthritis, she couldn't bend over and paint her toenails anymore. So my grandfather does it for her all the time, even when his hands got arthritis too. That's love." Rebecca, age 8

"Love is when my mommy makes coffee for my daddy and she takes a sip before giving it to him, to make sure the taste is OK." Danny, age 7

"Love is what's in the room with you at Christmas if you stop opening presents and listen." Bobby, age 7

A first-grade teacher gave each kid in her class the first half of a proverb, and then asked them come up with the rest. This is what some of the kids came up with:

As you shall make your bed so shall you *... mess it up*

Better to be safe than *... punch a fifth grader*

Strike while the *... bug is close*

It's always darkest before *...*
daylight-savings time

Don't bite the hand that *... looks dirty*

An idle mind is *... the best way to relax*

Where there's smoke, there's *... pollution*

A penny saved is *... not much*

***Two's company, three's** ... the Musketeers*

***Don't put off tomorrow what** ... you put on to go to bed*

***Laugh and the whole world laughs with you, cry and** ...you have to blow your nose*

***Children should be seen and not** ... spanked or grounded*

***You get out of something what you** ... see pictured on the box*

***When the blind leadeth the blind** ... get out of the way!*

We need to think more like kids—they know how to love life and have fun! That's why they have so little stress in life. It is a physiological fact that stress and laughter cannot occupy the same space at the same time. You cannot experience the state of stress while you are laughing. It's just not possible. Test it out sometime and see how true it is.

The average six-year-old laughs 300 times a day. The average adult laughs only 17 times a day. Adults subject themselves to more stress and anxiety. Kids don't walk around all stressed out—they can't, because they are too busy laughing. You can't be stressed when you're laughing.

Stress is one of the many factors that keep people from reaching their full potential and becoming successful in so many areas of their lives. Many people spend far too much time in a state of stress when they could be in a state of positive mental outlook, which will only increase the effectiveness they possess. If we could all learn to lighten up a little, maybe we can put what appears to be a stressful situation into its proper perspective. The good news is that you get to choose. Negative states don't just happen to you. In every situation in life you get to choose how you will respond. You may not always be able to control what happens to you, but as Charles Swindoll said "Only 10% of life is what happens to you, and 90% is how you choose to react to it."

Most people live their lives as if they have no choice in how they respond to conflict, adversity, or stress. They allow negative states to control their lives and the course their lives will take. People tend to choose a state that comes naturally instead of consciously choosing a state that will do themselves and everyone around them the most good.

Laughter crowds out any negative state you have entertained. Laughter creates an instant positive state of mind. If you can find the humor in anything, you can have a positive state at your fingertips. Or as Bill Cosby once said, "If you can laugh at it, you can survive it."

Dr. Lee Berk of Loma Linda University in California has studied the effects of laughter on the immune system. Studies prove that laughter lowers blood pressure, reduces stress hormones, and boosts the immune system. Additionally, laughter also triggers the release of endorphins, which are the body's natural pain killers. As a result, laughter creates a sense of well-being. Medical experts now believe that laughter can reduce pain and assist in the healing process. A good belly laugh is considered the equivalent to "an internal jogging." (So if you needed to lose weight, you could literally laugh your butt off!) Laughter provides good cardiac conditioning and helps muscles to relax after the laughter.

> *"Laughter is the closest distance between two people."*
> *— Victor Borge*

An interesting fact to consider: faking laughter will produce the same responses in the body as genuine laughter. The same endorphins are released and the same effects are created. So take advantage of this and go ahead and do your fake laugh at those dumb jokes people keep telling you! At least your body can benefit from them.

Life is too short to be so serious. Whatever it is that's going on in your life right now, you'll probably be able to laugh about it six months from now, so you may as well laugh about it *right now*. I read a quote once that pretty much sums it up: "A sense of humor reduces people and problems to their proper proportions." Or as Proverb 17:22 says: "A cheerful heart is good medicine but a crushed spirit dries up the bones." Keep a sense of humor and you'll keep your health.

> *"He who laughs, lasts."*
> *— Mary Pettibone Poole*

A sense of humor also helps us to overcome adversity. We all face adversity, but remember only 10% of life is what happens to you and 90% is how you choose to respond to it. You can either let adversity strengthen you or you can allow it to turn you into a wimpy whiney wuss. It's your choice.

One man faced some adversity that required a definite sense of humor. He was a photographer for a national magazine and he was assigned to take pictures of a huge forest fire. When he got out to the scene, the smoke was so thick he couldn't get any quality photos so he frantically called his home office and asked for an airplane. They assured him one would be waiting for him at the local airport. So he drove at top speed to the nearest airport and sure enough, there was a small plane warming up near the runway. He ran over, threw the door open, tossed in his gear and yelled, "Let's go, let's go, let's go!" The pilot quickly swung the plane into the wind, and off they went.

The photographer leaned over to the pilot and shouted, "Fly over to the north side of the fire and make three or four low level passes."

"Why?" The pilot shouted back. The photographer was getting frustrated. "So I can get the pictures. I'm the photographer and I need to get some stinkin' pictures. We don't have time for these questions—just do it!" There was a long silence. The pilot finally turned to the photographer and said, "Soooooooo... you're not the instructor?" Only 10% of life is what happens to you—90% is how you choose to react to it. A sense of humor covers a multitude of adversities!

THE BENEFITS OF A POSITIVE MENTAL OUTLOOK

The director of training at the University of Pennsylvania developed an Attribution Style Questionnaire (ASQ). It ranks people on an optimism and pessimism scale. Those who scored high in pessimism were high candidates for clinical depression. High scores for optimism were predicative of excellence from everything from sports to life insurance sales.

Met Life Insurance Company saved million of dollars in personnel selection by using this tool. They realized that someone who scored high on the optimism scale was more likely to succeed in sales than someone who scored high on the pessimism scale.

Another study examined ninety six men who had their first heart attack in 1980. Within eight years, fifteen of the sixteen most pessimistic men died of a second heart attack. But only five of the sixteen most optimistic men died of a second heart attack. There is much to be said of optimism and a positive mental outlook on life.

A psychological analysis of Mozart's correspondence shows that he was almost pathologically optimistic! He had an exuberant self-confidence that showed. Optimistic people who suffer setbacks in life tend to attribute those setbacks to *external* causes that are temporary and can be changed. Professor Andrew Steptoe of St. George's Hospital Medical School says that towards the end of Mozart's short life, when he suffered the deaths of four children, serious illnesses, and repeated professional and financial disaster, Mozart's optimism actually ***rose***!

Optimistic people usually have a sense of humor. Have you ever noticed that? If you've ever spent any amount of time around pessimistic people, you'll notice they don't seem to have much of a sense of humor at all. It's pretty difficult to have a positive mental outlook on life if you don't have a sense of humor and love what you do.

So here's your assignment: first of all, find a way to love what you do or find something else to do. If you're going to spend eight to twelve hours a day working at something, you should at least like what you do! It would be even better if you loved it. Yes, there will be tasks and projects and people problems that you don't like, but you should like your profession. Next, find a way to laugh every day. See the humor in things and more importantly, see the humor in yourself! Remember, life is too short to be so serious. Laugh, love, and lighten up!

Closing Thoughts...

If you are now offended after reading this book, it's probably due to one of three factors. People are generally offended for three main reasons:

1) You feel personally attacked
2) Something somebody says or does goes against your personal values
3) You just don't have a dang sense of humor!

So if something in this book offended you, it may be because you feel personally attacked as a result of my direct statements and observations (if someone says I am ugly, I get offended. It may be true, but I don't want to hear it). If you feel personally attacked, you may want to examine why that is. There may be things that have hit too close to home for you!

If the second reason applies to you, then I have said things that have gone against your values. You may not value responsibility, ownership, common sense, taking initiative, etc. If that's the case, all I ask is that you evaluate your value system and ask if your values have been serving you well and moving you towards success. There was a time in my life when my actions did not align with my values or my value system was messed up, and I did not experience the success God created me for. I had to examine my life, my motives, and my actions. I didn't like what I saw, so I made some serious changes!

If the third reason applies to you, then get a life! I mean, come on, if you don't have a sense of humor, you don't have much.

Well, there you have it folks—thirteen simple tips to getting a grip on a more successful life. As you can see, it's *not* brain surgery! You just need to find your purpose, get some passion, get off your butt, do the right thing, get some perspective, be a good steward, take ownership, exercise common sense, face your fears, stop being annoying, find a mentor, and pull the stick out and lighten up!

As you close this book today, remember: God has blessed America with amazing freedoms and unequaled opportunity for success in every area of our lives. If you can't make it happen here, the problem is probably not America, it's probably **YOU!** There are three types of people in the world: those who make things happen, those who watch things happen, and those who say, "What the heck just happened?" Be the first type—make things happen!

Other Books by Kimberly Alyn

How to Deal With Annoying People

Pillars of Success

101 Leadership Reminders

Public Speaking is Not for Wimps

My Favorite Sarcastic Sayings

Soar

How to Order Books by Kimberly Alyn

Log on to any of these web sites:

Amazon.com
BarnesAndNoble.com
KimberlyAlyn.com

OR CALL:

1-800-821-8116

For more information about Kim Alyn, her speaking services, and training workshops, log on to:

www.KimberlyAlyn.com

How to Schedule Kimberly Alyn for a Speaking Engagement

"Keynote speeches that give your audience a rude awakening they will welcome!"

Call:

1-800-821-8116

Or

Log on to:

KimberlyAlyn.com

Providing self-improvement with laughter and sarcasm!

How to Contact the Author

Phone: 800-821-8116

E-Mail: Kim@KimberlyAlyn.com

www.KimberlyAlyn.com